Bedford Square

Bedford Square

New Writing from the
Royal Holloway Creative Writing Programme

Foreword by **ANDREW MOTION**

JOHN MURRAY

© Tahmima Anam, Pat Borthwick, Neil Coulbeck, Ben Gardiner, Nina-Marie Gardner, David Hass, Myrlin Hermes, Doreen King, Adam O'Riordan, Sophie Orme, Rachel Thackray Jones, Harriet Thistlethwaite, Joe Treasure, Adele Ward, J. T. Welsch 2006

Foreword © Andrew Motion 2006

First published in Great Britain in 2006 by John Murray (Publishers)
A division of Hodder Headline

The right of Tahmima Anam, Pat Borthwick, Neil Coulbeck, Ben Gardiner, Nina-Marie Gardner, David Hass, Myrlin Hermes, Doreen King, Adam O'Riordan, Sophie Orme, Rachel Thackray Jones, Harriet Thistlethwaite, Joe Treasure, Adele Ward and J. T. Welsch to be identified as the Authors of the Work has been asserted by them in accordance with the Copyright, Designs and Patents Act 1988.

1

A CIP catalogue record for this title is available from the British Library

ISBN 0 7195 6822 6

Typeset by Servis Filmsetting Ltd, Manchester

Printed and bound in Great Britain by Clays Ltd, St Ives plc

Hodder Headline policy is to use papers that are natural, renewable and recyclable products and made from wood grown in sustainable forests. The logging and manufacturing processes are expected to conform to the environmental regulations of the country of origin.

John Murray (Publishers)
338 Euston Road
London NW1 3BH

Contents

Foreword

When I took over Malcolm Bradbury's Creative Writing MA course at the University of East Anglia ten years ago, I often met people who told me that writing couldn't be taught. Although they were perfectly comfortable with the idea that blossoming painters might go to art school, or actors to drama school, or dancers to ballet school, they assumed that writing 'just happened' – usually in an attic. It could not be improved (still less released) by conversations about practice and technique, by the formation of a mutually-supportive community, by the certainty of a concentrated year's work, or by advice about how to read more widely, stimulatingly and differently.

Eight years later, when I moved from UEA to start the new Creative Writing MA at Royal Holloway College, University of London, most of these doubters had fallen silent. The number of writing courses at British universities had grown from around ten to around fifty, and a significant number of graduates had emerged with agents, book contracts – and prize-garlands. But as one set of concerns was squashed, another group flourished. Are all available courses of equal value, and if not, what is the best model? How should creative writing be combined with study and analysis? How is it to be assessed within academies? Should the rise of MA creative writing courses be allowed to influence the way English (and maybe other subjects as well) is taught at undergraduate and school level?

These questions are central to the debate about the future of English studies. Interested parties such as the Poetry Society make their contribution by seeking to find ways (and funding) to get writers into schools on a more regular basis. Groups within the

Department for Education and Skills devise initiatives (such as 'English 21') to explore the implications of changes to the system. Although it'll probably be some time before any substantial revisions are enshrined in law, the outcome of these activities is already predictable. As we look into the future, we can see that sooner or later creative acts within schools and universities will be more intricately involved with critical acts. The education of our children will give proper space and encouragement to their imaginations, while equipping them with the necessary other skills – practical, functional and social, knowledge-based, and so on.

That's what I'd like to see, anyway – and when I turn the pages of this anthology, my hopes feel justified. It collects work produced by the inaugural members of the Creative Writing programme at Royal Holloway, and displays an exceptional range of talent – talent which has undoubtedly been stirred by the combination of creative and critical opportunities the course offers.

It has to be said that while such an assertion is heartening, it's also predictable. All leaders of all Creative Writing courses say something similar, when introducing the work of their students – and so they should. In my own case, I'm especially proud of the range of interests, stories and manners on show here. They run from shocking to familiar, from Bangladesh to LA (via the north and south of Britain), from experimental to traditional. And I'm also genuinely impressed by the mixture of technical dexterity and emotional commitment: these are all writers who understand that close attention to the nuts and bolts of writing, far from hampering strong feeling, is in fact the means by which strong feeling is dramatised.

But I'm also conscious that the value of the course extends beyond the qualities on display here. It appears in the workshops from which this work derives, in the independent contact that the students make with one another, in the unregistered thinking and reading which occurs alongside the assessed parts of the course. Taken together, these things describe an indefinite world of commitment and opportunity, which these poems and pieces of prose now validate in a wholly clear way. They are impressive and enjoyable. They represent a distinguished first-flowering for the Royal Holloway course. And they validate the reasons for setting up such a course in the first place.

ANDREW MOTION

Tahmima Anam

Tahmima Anam was born in Dhaka, Bangladesh, in 1975. _The Fasting Month_ is an excerpt from her novel-in-progress.

The Fasting Month

Dhaka, 1959

'Dear Milord. No. Dear yourlordship. Dear judge-saab. Dear Sir. My son Sohail is seven years old. He was born in 1952. July 8. I thought he would be a girl because I never felt tired, not once, even though my husband told me to restrestrest I was always running around, I even planted Hydrangeas that year. The day he came I sent for the midwife and she told me to squat and push and he didn't make a sound, just looked up and told me he was going to be my Lucky Boy. He looks just like me though he has inherited his father's unruly eyebrows; someday he will have to keep a special comb in his pocket for the express purpose. I tried to give him books for children, like *Five Go to Smuggler's Top* and *Mystery of the Flying Express*, but he climbed into my steel almirah and found *Wuthering Heights*, the copy I rescued the day my father had to sell his first editions to the debt collector with the missing teeth. My daughter, Maya, is dark and shiny, like her father, and already she has caused me tears because of her steely will. But she sings, your lordship, and not nursery rhymes, she has already started on the ghazals – she sings them as though she knows what they mean. Milord, your judgeship, the children are still in a state of shock at the untimely demise of their father. They need me, and their home, to ease the burden on their little hearts. Please, take pity. Take Pity. Takepity.'

As she rehearsed her speech, Rehana felt the thickness of her tongue and thought: the poets are wrong; the taste of defeat is not bitter, but salt. She stood perfectly still, here in front of her house, despite the sun blazing powerfully above her, unchecked, a punishment. She closed her eyes against it, against the moment, and was exactly this way, still and hot, her back to the gate, hearing nothing, not the chime of the Baby ice-cream man, or the lazy passing of stray rickshaws, or the cries of the vegetable and fish hawkers, when Moina came running from Mrs Chowdhury's house with a packet of Huq's Glucose Biscuits and a glass of water. As she ran, water escaped from one side of the glass and spilled on to the road, falling into a muddy trail that looked like spittle from the throat of a passing driver.

'Where have you left the children?' Rehana asked, shielding her eyes with a hand.

'With Mrs Chowdhury. You should eat something.'

'You know I can't do that.'

'So thin,' she heard Moina mutter, and she too expelled a tired breath at hearing the familiar phrase. Yes, she was thin. As thin as any woman could be without disappearing, she had overheard someone say once on a rare visit to the ginrummy ladies, snapping their card-wrists at the Dhaka Gymkhana Club (now admitting Indians and Dogs). But why should anyone be surprised? Still, she couldn't help feeling self-conscious, a little ashamed at the way people looked at her, as though they were afraid of contracting her misfortune. Her hair had grown long, and she had started wearing it loose, like a cape, covering the pointed shoulders, the jutting out clavicles, the cascade concealing her now tiny waist. Her eyes she could not hide; always big, they now dominated her face, great pools of black, reflecting nothing, only giving away what was within: a swell of held-in tears.

'I told you to stay with the children.'

'Mrs Chowdhury sent me. She says to drink some water.'

'You want me to break my fast in the middle of the day?'

'Mrs Chowdhury asks why she can't come to the courthouse.'

'I don't want Mrs Chowdhury. It's nothing. The lawyer says judges don't just give children away.'

But it wasn't just in the slight pause before she said it, or the way she held her arms so stiffly before her, or how she had pinned her sari so tightly that it had pressed flat against her forehead, or that she didn't complain of the heat, or even wipe the sweat from above her lip; it was entirely possible the judge would force Rehana to give up the children. She was a widow. She had no money. And here were her husband's elder brother and his pretty, film-star wife, generously willing to take them in.

As Moina walked away Rehana nervously plunged her hand into the purse slung across her shoulder and touched the photograph that lay within. She told herself she would not take it out again; it was already worn with her looking. Sohail in her arms, six months old, a fat, serious child. Rehana, looking straight into the camera, radiating an unchecked happiness. It was her husband's eye behind the lens, her son's weight against her chest, and joy, it seemed, was plentiful and cheap. She had not even given Sohail a black mark on the forehead to ward off the evil eye. Her own eyes were shiny, though she smiled so broadly they nearly disappeared, unlike her teeth, which were a bold white line in the photograph, a smooth canvas of pearl, except for one crooked tooth, the jutting-out left incisor, that gave her smile a feral quality, as though success had been hunted down with cunning and strategy rather than as it was really done, through fate, prayer and good fortune.

Before it turned the corner, Rehana heard the shiny newness of Faiz's car approaching, its shimmering white paint; she heard the hiss of the radiator grille, the throb of the engine. If she concentrated, she could even hear the pleasure Faiz took in sitting at the back with his wife and allowing the driver to follow the precise instructions that would deliver them to their destination.

The car stopped in front of the gate. Faiz waited while the driver hurried out and opened the door for him. Then he emerged, slow-motion, first with his polished shoe, then with the soft drape of his suit, to smile tightly and greet her.

'Rehana.'

'Brother,' she replied, moving toward the front seat.

'Sit at the back,' he insisted, trying to be kind, 'with your sister.' And he opened the door. As she lifted her sari to step into the car, Rehana noticed she had forgotten to change her rubber house-slippers. She thought about asking them to wait while she went back, but thought the better of it; it was getting late, they would roll their eyes impatiently and consider it another symptom. Of her misfortune.

It was a different world inside, close and airless and full of the collective scent of Faiz and Parveen. Rehana felt a quiet longing as she breathed in the heaviness of Parveen's perfume, the rounded, warm fragrance of Faiz's pomade. She imagined herself gripping the back of the car seat, her fingers pressing into the cream leather and releasing its fragrance, new and factory-bright, and saying, please, please don't take my children. I beg you. I beg you, for the sake of my dead husband – your brother, Faiz – to let my children be. With their mother. But instead she leaned awkwardly against the seat and tried to smile at Parveen.

Sitting beside her, Rehana felt brittle and small.

As Faiz's wife, Parveen was comfortable in shape as in position. A sharp face – chiselled, people had called it in her actress days – had softened and rounded out. She was still pale and delicate, only now she had the self-possession of a rich man's wife, the earlier fame a mere side note. Faiz refused any more films, and Parveen happily agreed, proud of her husband's will. But they had no children, and when she wasn't looking, Rehana saw sadness, and a kind of greed, etched on Parveen's prettiness.

'How are you today, Rehana? Feeling better?' Parveen asked.

Rehana wondered what answer she might give. They assumed it was a matter of resolve, like recovering from an illness. She started to reply, but changed her mind and said nothing, marvelling at her own inability to protest. She gazed at the road as they drove past her neighbours' houses, their shutters closed to the force of the afternoon sun.

'This heat!' Parveen said nervously. 'Only March and such heat!' She took out a red and blue polka dot fan from her handbag and began passing it back and forth across her face in quick, restless movements, each one punctuated with a fresh sigh.

Dhaka, the almost-city, shook beneath the wheels of the car. Made out of a colonial outpost, it was now called upon to perform the duties of a capital; it laboured under the weight of such expectation, and this gave the city its air of accident, the empty expanses of hastily covered delta swimming beneath the asphalt of new roads; large plots of land beside the signs of decay; newness and rot jostling for space.

As they left Dhanmondi, Rehana noticed a strange hush on the streets, as though everyone in the city had decided at once to stay indoors, or, if they had to venture out, to do so sparsely, in ones and twos. Even the air seemed not to move, the giant tamarind trees standing like sentinels on the side of the road.

'What's happened?' Rehana heard herself say.

'Martial law, sister! Don't you know?'

Yes, of course she knew; she just hadn't cared. So this was what it looked like: a quiet day, people's sorrows hidden inside them like relics.

'Putting order to the mess we have made of ourselves.'

Parveen looked out of the window and quickened the pace of her fanning.

'I don't care what anyone says,' Faiz continued, 'authority is what we need.'

Rehana had stopped listening; they were driving past Ramna racecourse. She couldn't see inside, but in the distance, where she knew there was a field, a pair of kites chased one another, floating and dipping through the air. Perhaps there was a breeze, she thought, and wished she could open the window.

'I don't think my brother would have disagreed,' Faiz said finally. Rehana wasn't sure. Unlike the men with whom he shared half-measures of whiskey-neat, Kazi wasn't interested in politics. He didn't get sweaty and energetic over the threat of divided Pakistan, or where all the jute money was being spent. He was absorbed with more practical matters: the growth of the children (measured alongside the garden wall), the protection of his wife (against illness, the sun, the gazes of men), the prevention of rainy days. The sidestepping of consequence.

They turned into the University compound and were met with loud political banners flapping from dormitory windows. 'Death to the Dictator!' they said. 'Democracy: People's Right' and 'Ayub Khan Must Go!' As they passed the Art College they saw a crude painting of a naked peasant whose back was bent before vast plains of paddy; men in army uniforms pointed guns at him; some whipped him, cutting crudely into the flesh. An enormous red sun dominated the background.

Faiz made a strange sound between a sneeze and a laugh, as though waiting for some provocation. With Rehana and Parveen remaining silent, he decided to sum it up:

'Dogs,' he said, to no one in particular.

Rehana took out her photograph and stared hard at it, willing her tears to remain exactly as they were, at the very corners of her eyes, balanced in the crease of her eyelids, but not spilling over on to her cheeks, not tracing the line of her nose, not falling on to her shoulder and blooming darkly on her white sari. Parveen said only one more thing during the ride.

'It's for your own good.'

A crowd had massed at the entrance to the courthouse: men, mostly, looking ferocious, raising their fists, their spittle flying into the air as they shouted to be let in. Rehana saw reporters, a flash, and felt something break underfoot as she stepped out of the car. There were men in green uniforms beating back the crowd, which heaved and swayed as one. Faiz held up his arms and towered above everyone else, making a path for Rehana and Parveen to push through. Parveen whispered, 'Are those cameras for me?' before remembering her last film had flopped almost ten years ago. Still, she shielded her face from the cameras with spread fingers, exposing the painstakingly lined eyes, drawn to look like a cat, or Audrey Hepburn. Rehana heard a few scattered words: dictator, coup, house arrest – before pushing through the doors and into the halls within. These were quieter, but still crowded, peons and clerks and petty officials making way for the lawyers who swayed brusquely through the corridors in their robes. Faiz was leading the way and Rehana followed through the maze of passages and verandas. She saw a young man who looked a little like Kazi, only younger, kneeling beside a bench and assembling a sheaf of papers. He was worried; a triangle of skin gathered at his forehead, and he was shuffling with the papers, glancing at them distractedly, arranging, rearranging. He dropped something with a clatter and said, dammit! under his breath, and Rehana frowned at hearing the word, though she still bent to pick it up. It was an elegant, expensive pen. The man thanked her, shame-faced, and muttered, 'My father's.'

'What are you doing?' she found herself asking.

'He's been jailed. Our assets are frozen.' He looked around and then said, in a lowered voice, 'My father was an MP. Ayub's been out to get him for years.'

'Your mother?'

'She's depending on me.' The triangle deepened. 'And you? Do you mind if I ask?'

Rehana closed her eyes for a moment, wondering if she should tell him. She wanted to reach out and pinch his forearm. 'It's nothing,' she said, for the second time that day.

'Well, good luck then. It's all up to the judge.'

No, she thought, rebuking him, up to God.

They came to a door labelled, in Urdu, FAMILY COURT, and as they passed through it, Rehana felt her knees grow cold and liquid. Her lawyer was waiting for her, a top-heavy man with a square face who had agreed to plead her case for a small sum. He flashed a smile at her, revealing a row of pointed teeth, and indicated she should sit down beside him. Rehana looked to Faiz, who had put on his gown and was frowning at the scene, as though there was a distant memory it did not match. The room was shabby, the red velvet covering the benches worn to a black shine, the ceiling displaying fans furry with dust. Even the light, from lamps attached to the panelled walls, only gave off a weak, shadowy light.

The judge came into the room and sat down unceremoniously on his chair, his only concession to the ritual the curled white wig he had hurriedly placed on his head. The grey ringlets appeared tattered and unruly, the judge's own black hair protruding from beyond the wig's reach. He pounded his gavel distractedly and got straight to the point.

'For what cause are you taking the court's time today?'

'Your lordship, Barrister Faizul Haque. My wife and I are applying for custody of the children of my brother, Kazi Ehsanul Haque, recently deceased, under section 146 of the Muslim Family Protection Act. We are moving to Karachi next month, sir, and wish to take the children with us.'

'Representing Mrs Haque, your lordship,' the lawyer said.

'Begum Rehana Haque?'

'Yes, your lordship,' Rehana replied, sounding strange to herself, as though she were someone else: a criminal, maybe, or a refugee.

'How long were you married, Mrs Haque?'

'Eight years, your lordship.'

'And you have two children?'

'Yes, your honour. Sohail and Maya. Seven and five.' She steadied her voice for the speech.

'The information is all in the brief, your lordship,' the lawyer interjected.

The judge riffled through some papers, cleared his throat, and began to read. 'Ah yes. Rehana Haque. Born in Calcutta to Farouq Ali,' he began. 'Lost his fortune before Partition. Family left Calcutta in '52, went to Karachi. Except you, Mrs Haque. You came to Dhaka to marry. Your father died shortly thereafter. Your sisters, Marzia, Rokeya, Zareena, all live in Karachi. No brothers. Is that right?'

'Yes, your lordship.'

The judge's face remained impassive. 'You live in Dhanmondi, Road 2?'

'Yes.'

'Your own house, Begum?'

'Yes.' Why wasn't he asking her anything about the children?

'Your husband owned Triple S Insurance, Limited. What is the state of the business?' For this he turned to the lawyer.

'Finished, your lordship. Without Kazi-saab, the business could no longer survive. But Mrs Haque will be getting a small allowance.'

'How much?'

'Fifty rupees a month, sir.' If this seemed a small sum to the judge, he did not say.

The judge turned to Faiz. 'And what is your prayer, Mr Haque?'

Faiz cleared this throat. 'Your lordship, these are difficult times,' he began solemnly. 'What would we be without the sanctity of the family? My brother and I were very close. Our parents, peace-be-upon-them, passed away many years ago. I never imagined Kazi would also pass before I did.' He paused for an expansive sigh. 'I helped him start the company. Built it from nothing. When he decided to marry Rehana on a whim, I did not protest. He was a gambling man, sir. Decided his fate by flipping a coin.'

'Is this relevant?' the lawyer protested.

'There is no doubt Rehana Begum is a devoted mother. But marriage, unlike life, should not be left up to fate. My brother did not know this. That is why he tossed a coin to decide whether he should marry.'

'Is this true?' the judge said, curious despite his hurry. Outside Rehana could hear the muezzin cry out from the courthouse mosque. The afternoon pressed upon her. She tried not to think of Mrs Chowdhury's Glucose biscuits.

'Yes, sir, very true,' Faiz continued. Rehana had heard the story a thousand times. Kazi, long overdue for marriage, had tossed a coin when presented with the proposal of marriage to a Begum Rehana Ali of Calcutta. When the shiny façade of the Islamabad Parliament looked up from the newly minted Pakistan rupee, he decided at once it was a clear sign. It was the last time he'd gambled: after marriage, Kazi became a nervous man, watchful over his wife, anxious about the children, devoted to the business and its underlying spirit: the calculation of risk and the avoidance of accident. But Faiz had not forgiven him for making his hasty, undirected decision, and then had frowned upon his brother's excessive concern for his wife.

The lawyer was standing up and raising his finger in protest as Faiz was finishing a sentence, '. . . doubts about her mental state.'

'Your lordship,' said the lawyer, attempting to sound authoritative, 'this allegation is completely baseless.'

'Let me hear it,' the judge interrupted. 'You will have your chance.' A slow yawn travelled through his face, though his curiosity had clearly been aroused; he suppressed a second.

'It was a terrible tragedy,' Faiz continued, smiling indulgently, 'but I am not sure she has handled it well. After all, she is very young.'

'Your lordship!' the lawyer shouted.

Faiz looked at Parveen with a look of regret, his arms held up in surrender. Parveen looked back at her husband and nodded serenely. 'Your lordship, it is with great regret that I say this. But Mrs Haque has conducted herself in a most inappropriate manner.'

'Please continue, sir.'

'Rehana – Mrs Haque – has refused to return to normal after my brother's death. She refuses to eat. She neglects the children. Sometimes they go to school without their uniforms.'

The judge took out a pen and began taking notes. 'Your lordship,' Rehana said, 'I can explain.'

'Yes, please, madam,' he replied, sounding like a very patient man.

Should she tell him about the children now? 'My husband died in Ramzaan. I was fasting then.'

The judge did not seem to understand. His eyebrows were still lifted in query.

'He died on a Friday,' she went on, 'and it was Ramzaan. And I am still fasting.' She saw the judge regarding her now, and noticing the narrowness of her wrists, the standing tendons of her neck. She saw him running through the possibilities: would she be an angry widow? A sad, weeping widow? A chest-beater? Ah yes, she heard him think to himself. Starving Widow. But what to do? Should she be pitied? Berated? Taught a lesson? Rehana could see the judge was not yet sure. She tucked her feet under the sari, hoping he would not notice the rubber slippers.

'You're fasting.'

'Yes.'

'As though it were still Ramzaan.'

'Yes.'

'Every day? Sunrise till sunset?'

'Yes, milord.'

'And the children?'

'The children are fine.'

'Yes, but what do they eat?'

She couldn't remember. She tried to conjure up an image of the children, sitting down at the table, munching on their favourite snacks. Then she remembered – yes, of course, 'Mrs Chowdhury. They have lunch with Mrs Chowdhury and her daughters.'

'Who is Mrs Chowdhury?'

'A neighbour, milord,' Faiz interjected, 'no relation to us.' When the judge stayed silent, Faiz continued, 'Milord, she fasts every day. She doesn't eat, doesn't drink. Sunup to sundown. And then she has iftar, as if it were Ramzaan – all the iftar foods – dates, fried eggplant, jalebis, everything. Is this normal, milord? And those poor children?' Faiz looked earnest, almost desperate. 'One day I went over and they were wearing their party clothes.'

'What do you mean?'

'They were dressed up!'

'Where were they going?'

'Nowhere, your honour. The poor lady goes nowhere.'

'They were doing a scene, milord.' How could she explain the fatherless mystery of her children? 'I just wanted to cheer them up.'

'A scene? What scene?'

'*The Importance of Being Earnest*, sir.'

'This is nonsense,' Faiz said. 'We are wasting the court's time.'

The judge's eyes were far away. 'Yes, it's true, we are in a hurry.' And then he said, a little regretfully, 'Mrs Haque, do you really think you can take care of these children by yourself? Do you have the resources? Have you thought about what your husband might want?'

At the mention of Kazi, the events of the last three months began to reassemble themselves. A quiet roar filled her ears as she remembered him, wrapped in his burial shroud, the cotton stuffed into his nostrils giving him a look of astonishment despite the dark lids, the shadowy mouth. And there were Maya and Sohail, still like a lake-top on a windless day, standing above him and saying nothing, staring, agape, at the picture of the dead man, their noses full of attar and incense burned to hide the rot; there were sweets in card-board boxes, packed and ready for the departing mourners, and a white curtain pinned across the lawn, separating the men from the women.

'I don't know,' Rehana heard herself saying, 'I don't know what he would want. He would want them to be safe, I suppose. Yes, he would want them to be safe.'

'It's not safe here,' Faiz said. 'That is why my wife and I are moving to Karachi.'

'You are willing to take care of these children?'

'I will love them as my own, your lordship.'

'Mrs Haque, perhaps this will give you a chance to recover.'

She hadn't taken the children anywhere. She had been reluctant to admit their father was really dead. She had refused to explain Heaven and Hell to them. And there was that time Maya had found her sprawled underneath the garden tap. She nodded to the judge.

The judge nodded back.

Immediately, she changed her mind. 'Oh no, you can't do it! Oh God, oh God, oh God.'

'Please, Mrs Haque, compose yourself.'

Compose. Now she was a Hysterical Widow.

'You will take these children to Karachi?' the judge asked Faiz.

'Yes, your lordship. There are excellent schools in Karachi. And none of this revolution-business.'

Karachi was so far away. It was on the other side of a thousand miles of India. What a map they have drawn us, Rehana thought, and if I had known it would put a continent between me and my children, I would have killed that mapmaker myself. My son is seven years old. Seven years old. He was born on July 8, 1952. If only they had let her begin with that.

But it was too late. She looked to the right, past the lawyer and into the corridor, where the painted courthouse pillars gleamed in the afternoon sun, and to her left, where a magpie had paused on the high branch of a tamarind tree. One for sorrow, Rehana said to herself. Two for joy. She heard the judge's decision, though she pretended not to. If she didn't hear the words, perhaps what followed would not follow – the judge's gavel would not be pounded; he would not rise as though his business was finished; a flat, unpleasant smile would not make its way to Faiz's mouth; Parveen's heels would not fall satisfyingly on to the marble floor, and Rehana would not crumple, passing the lawyer's outstretched hand, avoiding the bench that might have broken her fall; her sari would not have inflated around her knees like a balloon; and yet, the moment did pass, the judge did his duty, Faiz and Parveen theirs, and Rehana fell, as she might, at the knowledge that she had given her children away.

The lawyer made a final attempt to change the judge's mind. 'Your lordship,' he cried out, 'please do not make a hasty decision!'

From the ground where she lay Rehana heard the judge exhale a long, tired breath. She heard it in snatches: 'This court's time has already been wasted . . . martial law . . . country . . . chaos . . .' And then: 'That is all. Dismissed.'

Outside the courthouse Rehana bought two kites, one red and one blue, from Khan Brothers Variety Store and Confectioners. The kites were made of thin, translucent parchment paper, and were held together by slender bamboo reeds crossed in the middle and tied with a length of jute. Fastened to these were small, tightly wound balls of string. Paper ribbons hung festively from the corners. Rehana tucked the packets under her arm and hailed a rickshaw. As she was climbing in she saw the lawyer running towards her. His belly stayed rigid as the rest of him wobbled.

'Mrs Haque, I am very sorry.' He sounded sincere.

Rehana couldn't bring herself to say it was all right.

'You must find some money. That is the only way. Find some money and then we will try again. These bastards don't move without a little grease.'

Money. Rehana stepped into the rickshaw and lifted the hood over her head. 'Dhanmondi,' she said, her voice in a thin quiver. 'Road number 2.'

When she got home the children were sitting together on the sofa with their knees lined up. Maya's feet hovered above the floor. Sohail was looking down at his palms and counting very small lines. He saw Rehana and smiled but did not rise from his chair, or cry out, as Maya did, 'Ammoo! Why were you so long?'

Rehana decided it would not be wise to cry in front of the children, so she had done her crying in the rickshaw, in sobs that caused her to hold on to the narrow frame of the seat and open her mouth in a loud, wailing O. The rickshaw puller had turned around and asked, as if he was genuinely concerned, whether she would like to stop for a cup of tea. Rehana had never stopped by the roadside for a cup of tea. She refused him mutely, wondering if he had children, a thought that made her lean her head against the side of the rickshaw hood and knock, repeatedly, in time to the bumps on the road. Now, confronted with the sight of them, she fought the pinch in her jaw and the acrid taste that had flooded her mouth. She fought the fierce stinging of her eyes, the closing of her throat, the tremble of her lip. She fought all of these as she handed them the wrapped-up, triangular packets.

'Thank you, Ammoo-jaan,' Maya said, tearing into hers. Sohail did not open his. He rested it on his lap and stroked the brown wrapping. Then he bit down on his lip and stared at his mother.

'You are going to live with Faiz chacha,' Rehana said evenly. 'In Karachi.'

'Kra-chee!' Maya said gleefully.

'I'm so sorry,' Rehana said to her son.

'When will we come back?'

'Soon, I promise.' Pray to God, she wanted to say, but couldn't.

'When will we go?'

'They are coming for you tomorrow morning.'

'Please, ma. Please, I don't want to.'

Rehana bit down on her tongue. 'You have to go,' she said. 'Go and be brave. You can fly your kite, *beta*, and I will see it, all the way from Karachi. It's a very special kite. You have to be very good. Very good and very brave. Only the bravest children get windy days. And one day it will be so windy you will fly all the way back to me. You don't believe me? Wait and see.'

Neil Coulbeck

Neil Coulbeck is married, with two adult sons. He has spent most of his working life in the City of London, but is now a self-employed author. *Old War Stories* is set in the Second World War and interweaves events in the lives of English and German characters.

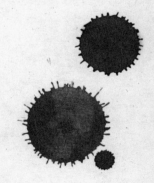

Old War Stories

Home, October 1942

Anna breathed in sharply as she splashed cold water up from the wash basin. She saw her modest nipples pucker and laid her palms across her breasts, willing them to take shape, like Kristina's, heavy with their own weight. She sighed testily, let her shoulders sag, gave a faint shrug and tossed her head; then she lathered coal tar soap in the basin before washing behind her ears and under her arms. She dried herself with the blue hand towel, cleaned her teeth through foaming white powder, patted her cheeks and ran a brush vigorously through her sleek, dark hair, hoping it would shine today.

She knew Rolf had come home during the night: her mother had received a letter a few weeks ago, telling them he would soon be back from Africa, although he couldn't say exactly when; there had been banging at the door in the early hours, the clattering of boots and thump of heavy weights in the narrow hallway; the sound of her mother on the floor below opening the bedroom door and creaking downstairs; hushed greetings and insistent whispering. She had got up and gone to the landing, seen the lights switched on two floors below, padded to the lower landing, leaned down and called out.

'What's happening?'

'Go to bed, you'll find out in the morning.'

'Is it Rolf?'

'Do as I say. Growing girls need sleep. Mind you don't get splinters in your feet.'

'Is he back?'

'Anna! How many more times? You'll wake your Nanna and catch your death.'

She wasn't her proper Nanna and the weather had been very mild, but it was never worth arguing with Mother: she just got upset; she had enough on her hands already without disobedient children. Anna had stood for a moment alone in the dark with one hand on the wooden orb at the bottom of the banister. The muffled plumbing gurgled like a well-fed baby and bedsprings whinged in Stefan's room, while in Nanna's it was still. She had flicked her hair and sauntered back up the bare wooden stairs, then taken the last few two at a time, her thin bare thighs sensing the cold draught beneath her nightie. As she was passing Stefan's room he called out in a raised whisper.

'Is it Dad?'

'Yes, but Mummy says we can't see him.'

'That's just stupid.'

'She means it for the best.'

Anna defended her mother from criticism: she wasn't his sister, only his stepsister, and she stood up for her own, as was only natural; he did the same with his father.

She had gone back into her tiny room, anxious not to wake Nanna and cause ructions. She had slipped quietly into the soft, white sheets, already cooled, and lain awake for most of the night listening and thinking: what would it be like now Rolf was back home? Did he have a medal? Would she tell Rosa, when she saw her after the morning break, and what did Rosa want to see her for, when she was normally so careful to keep an even distance between herself and all the pupils, because she knew they all wanted her to like them more than any of the other teachers? When would victory finally be declared? What would Krissie think?

Daydreaming wouldn't do: Anna pulled on her vest, stepped into her cotton dress, buttoned it up and buckled the belt. She would have liked to show off her uniform to Rolf, but they weren't on parade today. As she pulled on her socks, she thought for a moment how delicious it would feel to roll silk stockings up her calves and over her knees, to pause before a full-length mirror, dab powder on her cheeks and lipstick on her mouth, squirt a dash of perfume behind her ears and sashay down the stairs to greet Rolf: then he would look at her and see how much she had changed in the three years he had been away. She scolded herself and decided what the punishment should be; she would put no jam on her breakfast roll: that seemed just.

She knew she was leaving little Anna behind: boys had started looking at her this summer at the bathing lake; now men on the street eyed her, until she looked down and they knew she'd noticed them. She wasn't like Kristina, tall, sleek and blonde as one of the women in the newsreels displaying the virtues of exercise, but she was pleased with her small, slim, dark looks. She liked to shimmy her hair, to shoot glances, to slope her shoulders: agile and elusive, that was the Anna she wanted to be; she would be different from Kristina, not so beautiful but quicker, cleverer . . . what worried her sometimes was that she also knew she would simply never be *good*, like Krissie was.

She came on to the landing at the same time as Stefan. His knees showed beneath his brown shorts and the top of his socks cut into his calves, like string tied round a boiled joint.

'Ladies first.'

He flushed as his voice sharpened on 'Lay-' before '-dees': it had tormented him by breaking later than his friends and still betrayed him when he was embarrassed. He lowered his eyes as she walked by, then followed her down the stairs with the hefty gait he thought went with his uniform. She wondered if he was looking forward to seeing Rolf again: it didn't look it; perhaps he had started to enjoy being the only man in the house.

Mother must have been up for ages. She was on her knees in the scullery, scrubbing hard at the clay-fired tiles, leaning her weight through both hands into the stiff brush: when she looked up her face was paler than usual and the dark smudges at the inner corners of her eyes had dug down into her cheeks. She stood up slowly when Anna came in and eased her back.

Breakfast was laid out on the deal table in the middle of the kitchen, with a cloth and the best crockery. Anna sniffed the bitter tang of coffee . . . coffee?! She looked at her mother who gave a thin smile as she wrung her floorcloth into the sink.

'He brought some back. Italian. God knows how.'

Anna was dunking her roll in warm sugared milk when Rolf came into the room, unshaven, wearing a vest and his army trousers, the braces dangling loose and low like the arms of an orang-outang. She saw her mother frown at Rolf and steal a look at her. Rolf stopped by the door, gazed at Anna, at Stefan and then again at Anna. She could see him noting the changes in them both, but most of all in her. He raised his hand to his shoulder and massaged the flab uncomfortably, crushing a few sparse hairs, stiff and prickly as cactus spikes. He looked doubtfully at Eva.

'I didn't realise . . . excuse me . . . just a moment.'

He retreated quickly, looping his braces over a wrist as he made for the stairs. Anna ate her breakfast and listened to him shuffling heavily around in the bedroom over their heads. She denied herself apricot jam, even though she realised that the sin remained a sin whatever she did, unless she repented of course, which her conscience said she didn't, and that she ought to anyway as there was hardly any left. There was never much conversation at the Doppler table. She could remember her father when she was young, always talking passionately about this or that, things Anna hadn't understood, but which she now guessed had been politics: her mother simply bustled about, making sure they all ate properly; her silences grew more palpable year by year.

When Rolf came back down he was hoiking his braces over a clean grey collarless shirt. He had shaved hastily, nicking a pimple on his plump cheek, where he'd stuck a scrap of cigarette paper. Eva brought the white porcelain coffee pot from the dinner service over to the table and nodded to him.

'That's better.'

Rolf rubbed his hands and walked round the table.

'Well, children. Stefan!'

Stefan stood up clumsily, bracing himself as if he might be coming to attention. His father stopped in front of him, bemused, made as if to embrace him, then offered his hand, which, after hesitating, Stefan took. Rolf's arm flailed as it pumped his son's too manfully.

'Very smart. Quite the young man.'

'Yes.'

Stefan looked as if he wanted to say more, but couldn't think of anything, so he sat down again.

'And Anna, such a big girl now.'

He turned to her and bent to kiss her on the cheek. She smelt the tang of his sweat under the shaving cream and ducked away; she heard his lips brush her hair and felt them through the black curtain which had fallen in front of her ear. He stepped back and Anna felt a pang of pity; she had quite liked Rolf, who didn't mind her being more intelligent than him and Stefan, but living in the same house now that she was grown up was obviously going to be difficult for both of them, especially as he wasn't her real father. Three years ago when she was still a little girl it had been different, but now everything was changing. She watched Rolf stomp to the sideboard: he seemed fatter than before, and walked ponderously, like a deep sea trawlerman who has just set foot on shore.

'Presents for the children. From Africa. Here you are, my lad.'

Rolf handed Stefan a curved dagger in an ornamental sheath and Stefan grinned with pleasure: Anna thought that she should have come first, as the lady.

'Thanks, Dad.'

Stefan slipped the dagger out and they all admired its slim, glistening blade; he put his thumb to it and smiled as he felt how sharp it was.

'It's Arabic.'

'It's fantastic.'

'And for Anna, by courtesy of General Rommel, something else to read . . .'

He handed her a book with dark blue marbled covers. She looked inside, inspecting the Ex Libris label and the name in the top right-hand corner. On the facing page was some neat pencil writing in English: she could grasp only odd words: it frustrated her because she wanted to understand it all.

*'Why . . . write . . . clarity . . . power . . . write . . . things so deep
and . . . poetry can . . . not . . .? Poets . . . boundaries . . . shame
. . . say what they . . .? . . . hope not. PW 6/42'*

Rolf was eager for her response, proud of his gift.

'It must have belonged to an English officer. He's written things
inside . . . in pencil . . . we can rub them out.'

Her indifference obviously dismayed him: good; she meant to
unsettle him.

'You like poems, don't you?'

She pretended to read on, hunching a little when he bent back
down to point with his stubby forefinger.

'Look, it's taken some battering. He must have had it with him
in the desert, then in hospital.'

Anna looked at the scuffed cover, bruised and wrinkled at one
corner like a bashed pear, but said nothing. She thought the dagger
was a far superior gift, probably much more expensive, and not so
obviously used: it occurred to her that he might not have bought
the book at all, but found it; she could get it from Rosa in the
library, if she wanted, anyway.

'Who was he? Powl . . . Voolsley?'

She leafed back and forwards through the book, the pages light
and dry as thin toast.

'I don't know. Wounded, I expect, or killed. It wasn't a picnic,
Tobruk.'

He straightened and addressed them all, as if it were a little
school assembly.

'We gave them a pasting, I can tell you. They didn't know what
had hit them. First bombers, then artillery, and finally the tanks.
Like boxing: two to the body and one to the chin; one, two, three.'

He didn't look or sound as if he'd ever been in the ring. He must
have heard someone in a bar. Anna flipped back to the front and
scanned the first page:

ANNUNCIATION

(The words of the angel)

You are closer to God than we;
We are all far from him.
Your hands are wonderfully
Blessed; delicate, firm, slim.
No other woman, only you
Shows beauty in her sleeves.
I am the day, I am the dew,
But you, you are the trees.

I'm tired now, I've come a long way,
Forgive me, I forgot
What I was told to say today
When I left his hot
Golden sunlight presence, spinning
Through space to find your peace.
See: I may be the beginning
But you, you are the trees.

. . .

I may gust through the green
But you, you are the trees.

She wanted to carry on but stopped herself and laid the book on the bread crumbs by her plate; she would read it on her own later: pleasures tasted best private and deferred.

'Thank you, Sir.'

She hadn't meant to say Sir, but she had stuck on 'Father', which is what she used to call him when she was younger, because she'd already called her father 'Daddy' so he couldn't be that – 'Mr Doppler' made her sound like a maid . . . she didn't dare say

'Rolf' . . . and to use no name seemed rude . . . but why was he so crestfallen?

'What's all this Sir about? Just because I'm a Sergeant now. My own daughter doesn't need to call me Sir.'

Anna saw Stefan sit up at Sergeant, a smidgen straighter in his chair. She didn't say she wasn't his daughter, but guessed that her silence as she stood up from the table would prompt the thought in all their minds.

'I have to go. I'm meeting Kristina. I can't help in the shop this afternoon, Mummy. Rosa's arranged for us to help with the harvest on the estate, instead of athletics.'

'Rosa, Rosa, that woman, she's all I hear about. All right, dear. Anyway, Rolf is back now. He'll be running the shop again.'

Anna saw Rolf sit down uneasily. In the living room she took longer than she needed to gather things for her satchel and kit bag. She heard Rolf in the kitchen, pleading slowly and reluctantly like a boy who needs to be excused.

'I'm sorry, Eva. I'm back at work the day after tomorrow. Leipzig . . . it's a dead cushy number. I thought you understood.'

'The only thing I understand is that women do everything while you men swan around in the goddam army. We work, we bring up the children, we keep the house. Everything.'

'Eva, Eva, please, you mustn't talk like that. The war will soon be over, then everything will be all right.'

Stefan came into the living room and raised his eyebrows.

'They're off already.'

Rolf's voice was louder now, and deeper.

'I have to go. It's my duty.'

'Duty, duty, duty. I'm so tired of duty. We can't live just on duty.'

'Yes, I know, you're right, but what can I do?'

Anna followed Stefan down the stairs and into the shop. A wishy-washy morning light was soaking through the adverts stuck to the inside of the windows and on the lowering dark shelves bottles gleamed like false teeth under a bedside lamp. They hurried past the counter, through display tables and stacked boxes, under one of Mother's medical posters, the one with a huge staring Hygiene Eye, as wide and bright as a debutante's dropped with belladonna, set in a starry firmament above a colonnade labelled:

Undying Nation Exhibition
German Hygiene Museum Dresden
NSDAP Department for National Health

They came out with a clinging of the customer bell into the brighter street. The CLOSED card bobbed behind the window of the door for a few moments after they had left, then swayed from side to side like a popped up jack-in-the-box before it came to rest, waiting for Eva to flip it round and unbolt ready for another day's business, as the sign at the front advertised:

DOPPLER — HOUSEHOLD GOODS
HOME AND COLONIAL

Coffee	Household soap
Tea	Medicinal soap
Chocolate	Disinfectants
Sugar	Washing products
Biscuits	Defumigants
Tinned goods and packets	Surgical requirements
Spices	Bandages
Wines and spirits	Oils
Medicinal and dessert wines	Perfumes
Red and white table wines	Baby foods

Fruit and vegetables
All kinds of pipe tobacco and cigarettes

Outside it felt as warm and damp as the scullery on washing day: Anna looked up at the low clouds strewn like soap suds over the draining board; a window needed opening to let some fresh air in. In the square people were hurrying about their business: there was no time to gaze through the yellowing canopy of the limes, beyond the stone carvings under the eaves, up at the sky. A long queue stood waiting for the next tram: most of the men wore a uniform of some sort; the women wore coats and respectable hats.

Stefan headed down to the boys' school whilst Anna turned up the hill, walking briskly past the blocks of flats, residences and family homes towards Kristina's house, one of the nice villas near the top with a view back out across the city. Krissie was waiting at the gate, leaning casually against the metal post with her satchel on her back, her bag slung over her shoulder.

'You're late.'

'My Dad's just back from Africa.'

At school she called him that, to avoid any fuss. Krissie fell in alongside Anna, turning down the avenue towards the school.

'Is he wounded?'

'Of course not. He's too old, that's all.'

'He's not as old as my Dad.'

'He's going to be a guard.'

'What's it like in Africa?'

'He didn't say. He brought Stefan a dagger.'

'A dagger?'

'It's horrible. It's Arab.'

'Urr.'

'He got me a book.'

'What is it?'

'Only poetry.'

They walked on. Anna was proud to walk with Krissie, the most beautiful girl in their year, the best at games, the one everybody liked, the captain of almost everything, the class, the troop, and all the sports teams. The other girls, filing towards the gates in little groups, looked at her with envy and respect, Kristina's best friend Anna, otherwise far too smart to be popular.

Rosa was on duty in the yard, patrolling with her hands behind her back. She moved quickly to interrupt a quarrel between two of the senior girls: there was never trouble in the yard when Rosa was on duty; everyone responded to her sense of what was right and the air of purpose in the smallest things she did. She continued her round, stopping to greet a pair of first years saying goodbye to their mothers. She wasn't as tall as Krissie and craning her neck forward to speak down to the new girls she reminded Anna for a moment of a crow pecking at a worm. As they walked past her shooing a gang of boys away from the gate, Kristina saluted and Anna followed suit. Rosa smiled and returned the greeting.

'Good girls!'

The moment of pleasure lasted Anna through the whole of the German period when the teacher, a doddery old man exempted from service because of his weak chest, asked some of the girls to read out their essays on the subject of 'Harvest Time'. Everyone knew Anna's would be the best, but he was new to the class and didn't get round to her. She stared out of the high window, wondering if anyone lived in the square stone tower she could see above the trees, with a steeply pitched roof, turrets and big old-fashioned clock. She had grown out of imprisoned princess stories ages ago: maybe there was a dwarf who maintained the clock, poking his oil can into its whirling cogs and wiping the spout clean with a greasy rag . . . She sighed, plonked her elbow on the desktop and rested her chin on her hand, her shoulder sloping away from the class. She watched the slowly shifting patterns of the clouds, hoping the sun would break through by the afternoon.

'At harvest time we thank God for all the gifts of the earth and all the good food . . . Harvest time is the time of year when everybody works hard together . . . For the German people harvest time is one of special celebration . . .'

In her own essay she had tried to be realistic, talking about the sunshine on the cornfields, the warm breezes, the ripening grapes in the vineyards, but also stressing the right theme, natural fertility. She had written it to please Rosa; she didn't care what the smelly old man thought about it: if he asked her, she would say she hadn't done it because her father had just come back from Africa, fighting for Rommel . . . he wouldn't challenge that.

Krissie stood up and pushed her long, blonde hair back with both hands as if she were about to dive into the lake, before picking up her exercise book. She halted as she read her effort: it was jumbled, trite and only just long enough. The teacher thanked her, unsure how to deal with a girl who stood as tall as him in grey socks and a check print pinafore dress, which made her look like an adult doll. The class smiled with relief: Kristina's strengths lay elsewhere, outdoors on the playing fields, in the gym, at camp and on the parade ground. Kristina grimaced at Anna when she sat down, as if to say that she had got through it, but Anna would have done much better: well, she would; they all knew that.

The second lesson was Frau Lenz and Anna had to concentrate. She wasn't the best at maths: that was little Julia in the front row, who couldn't even swim; but she was quick enough if she kept her mind on it, and she desperately wanted to do her best in front of Frau Lenz. She was more rigorous than Rosa, fair but unforgiving in her judgements, unwilling to ignore weaknesses, just because you meant well. Such insistent justice tormented Anna, who wanted to be told she was better than she was. She worked hard all lesson and earned an encouraging smile from Frau Lenz when she submitted her painstaking algebra.

'Just one slip, my dear, here in the second line.'

Anna's lower lip quivered like a jelly slammed on the table by a sulky maid. She walked quickly back to her desk, avoiding Krissie's look of sympathy. How could it all be wrong when she had made only one mistake? It wasn't fair when everything else was right. She had very nearly done everything properly and she didn't want to be a swot like Julia, she was Krissie's best friend and she was sure that Rosa liked her as much as she liked Krissie, maybe even more.

As break time approached Anna's mouth began to dry. She hadn't told Krissie she was seeing Rosa, so she slipped out of class ahead of her and lost herself in the throng going down the stairs, then ducked down the long, dingy corridor towards the library. She stopped herself running as she passed a teacher, but walked as fast as she could. In the library she paused at the hush, the smell of varnish, old leather and stale paper, then hurried on through the shelves of bound volumes with gold titles, past the plaster bust of Goethe which sat on an oak table under the leaded window, the white head dappled pink, blue and green by the light from the stained-glass picture window of Tristan and Isolde. She stopped at the wooden door marked LIBRARIAN, hesitated, steadied her breathing, and then knocked, respectfully but firmly.

'Come.'

Rosa was sitting at her desk by the window, marking work. She looked up and nodded Anna to the seat in front of her. In Rosa's private office a salute seemed out of place and Anna simply sat.

'Just a minute.'

Anna sat while Rosa scanned the script in front of her, making red jots in the margin. She looked round at the cramped room, stuffed with books: history and poetry on makeshift shelves beside the desk, and a pile of modern editions on the table: *The Concept and Form of the Hitler Youth* . . . *Heritage, Race, People* . . . *The Sacrificial Way* . . . Rosa taught history, but often quoted poetry to prove her points, a combination Anna adored as much as blackcurrants and cream. She wondered what was in those other books, printed in bold, gothic script.

'Well, young lady?'

'You wanted to see me.'

'Yes. But how are you? How's your mother coping with the shop?'

'My stepfather's just got back from Africa. But he's going away again. Mother manages all right. I help her in the afternoons when we're not with you.'

'And Nanna?'

'Oh, Nanna's fine. She moans about her food.'

'We all have to make sacrifices.'

'Yes. He brought me a book.'

She took the Rilke from her satchel and passed it across. Rosa turned it in her small hands as deftly as a piece of floured pastry, and opened it.

'Is it from England?'

'He said he found it in a British hospital. In Africa. I think he said . . . Trobuk?'

'Tobruk.'

Rosa nodded as if it was famous and she knew all about it, like Verdun or Austerlitz.

'Be careful: enemy objects must be treated with caution.'

Anna loved the rare smiles Rosa gave when she was saying something in a way which left you wondering if she really meant it; she sometimes thought she did it just for her, because she knew she would be the only one to notice: secrets between the two of them, as thrilling as the teaspoons of icing sugar she and Krissie had shared in a midnight feast when she had stayed with her one night before the war and they had crept down the wide, carpeted staircase of the villa to raid the larder.

'And this, this is especially dangerous.'

She handed it back to Anna.

'Go steady with him, at your age. Small amounts. Like mustard.'

Anna put the book in her satchel, resolving to read it in bed that night, now she knew it was pernicious.

'I think you and I understand each other in some ways rather well, don't we, Anna, and you have a certain maturity of outlook, if I may say so, for a girl of your years.'

The flattery was as sweet to sip as lemon sherbet from a straw.

'You're all still very young, though. Most of the other girls haven't started to think yet. But you have. I'm concerned you're not playing the role you should in class. You're . . . taciturn . . . withdrawn.'

Rosa paused to screw the black top back on the golden nib of her pen.

'With your intelligence, you should be making a lively contribution. School is part of society and we all have to learn to participate.

I think your friendship with Kristina is distracting both of you. You're as thick as thieves this year.'

Anna was puzzled: she and Krissie had grown closer over the summer, swimming together in the warm afternoons and talking for hours in the shade of the birch trees by the lake, but Krissie was still the leader of the class; Rosa must have some other concern, but she couldn't see what it was.

'I think you should consider this friendship and its wider implications. Kristina is a wonderful girl, but she is physical and you are much more . . . intellectual. You need some companionship of another kind: I don't suppose you read poetry with Kristina?'

'She isn't interested in that sort of thing.'

'Precisely. And you are. As am I, of course.'

Anna sensed a new direction in the conversation and her heart thumped: was Rosa trying to wrest her away from Kristina to herself? Anna was excited at the thought, but also scared. How could she be friends with a teacher? . . . Obviously not in the way she was friends with Kristina, and she couldn't imagine what it would involve.

'Would you like to bring your book one day and read some poetry together? You could come to see me at the weekend. After the harvest work we'll deserve some . . . spiritual relaxation.'

A smile flitted over Rosa's face, as swiftly as a martin, come and gone.

'Yes. Thank you.'

'Sunday afternoon?'

'Yes.'

'At three o'clock, then, I'll expect you.'

'Yes. Thank you.'

There was a long silence in the stuffy office.

'And think about what I said – the implications . . . the consequences . . . I'm sure you understand what I mean, a clever girl like you.'

'Thank you.'

'Don't keep saying thank you. You'd better go now. Break's over.

We'll see each other in the fields this afternoon. It looks as though it might be harvest weather.'

Outside the clouds were lifting and patches of pale blue appeared behind the white and grey.

'Dismissed.'

Anna walked out in a daze, unsure what had been said and agreed, and what mysterious contracts had been entered into. She sat through two hours of home and hygiene education without registering anything, even when the visiting specialist described the threat of plague, cholera, typhus and tuberculosis, which came from dirty foreign people, and in a softer voice the risk of other nameless, more terrible diseases which came from sinful behaviour: at this point the class had grown still, as if it were in church or awaiting the start of a particularly difficult exam with lots of long equations. She would normally have been interested, because her mother worked at the Hygiene Museum before the war, then had to give it up when Rolf went away and wasn't there to mind the shop every other afternoon, one of the things Eva held against him, not to mention the authorities . . . today she couldn't concentrate: the woman droned on about the threat to national health of weak and inferior people who bred more quickly than proper Germans and threatened the future of the race; Anna yawned.

Ben Gardiner

Ben Gardiner was born in 1979 and is a member of C.A.M.
This is an excerpt from his novel-in-progress *They Said It Was Beautiful, But Jack Wasn't So Sure.*

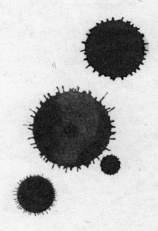

They Said It Was Beautiful, But Jack Wasn't So Sure

It doesn't matter all that much because it isn't really a story to tell. But he's twenty-three and she's twenty-three and they met through a friend. Fours years later and the friend hasn't introduced them to anyone else. If you were forced to tell the story then you might mention how they rent a house in the town where they work – would anyone remember what their jobs were if that were mentioned too? You could add that the house has one main bedroom and one spare but that they're not too happy with the kitchen. The bedroom has one wardrobe for her and one for him, and the bed is in the middle on the back wall. On either side of the bed are matching bedside tables on which they both keep alarm clocks, since neither had wanted to lose their own. In the drawers they keep plastic dogs; little notes; postcards and key rings: peculiar and personal shavings they have nowhere to put, but somehow can't put out. And that maybe it's telling, that all you could think to tell is the positioning of their furniture. And their names maybe. He is called Jack, she is called Jane, and that is that and there's little more to it.

Maybe it would be better to talk of Mr Jacobs. It is his house after all. Having heard that Jane was looking for a house to live in, he had offered to move out and let her have his. He had reasoned that the house was too big for him to live in by himself; Jane had reasoned that you shouldn't look a gift-horse in the mouth. Jack had reasoned that when an old horse suddenly starts giving gifts to a girl, it wasn't its mouth you should be worried about – but when he'd heard how cheap the rent was he'd opted to close his eyes. However, on the day of the switch, Mr Jacobs discovered that while the first house was too big for him, the second was too small. His new residence, it seemed, would only accommodate a box of books and a few changes of clothes. So while the body of Mr Jacobs relocated comfortably into the second place, his spirit remained behind to help Jack and Jane fill the first. Mr Jacobs claimed that he found the divorce from all but his essential worldly possessions quite uplifting. Although he undermined this nod at minimalism, by being unable to decide for certain what those essential possessions were. As a consequence, Jane is summoned to his Ark every few days, ferrying various possessions over and loaded up with various possessions to take back.

'When you take his stuff you should leave through the back door and return by the front, we're living in the mouth and arse of that guy's life,' Jack often says, wrapping the words in a smile like a rickety Trojan horse.

In tiptoe steps they have slowly erected their own little tent within his museum. In the lounge, each of the thirty foreign ornaments, from each of the thirty foreign countries Mr Jacobs has known, is obscured by one of the thirty souvenirs quickly collected by Jack and Jane. His decanter of whiskies and boxes of cigars are covered by the green patterned throw they've borrowed off Jane's aunt; the end of which tails down his oak wood chest and veils his antique umbrella stand – the umbrellas moved to the porch to be used when it rained. Each of his paintings of Victorian London finds itself inhabited by gaudy cartoon characters, drawn in pen on the Perspex covers they've attached. In the bedroom, his broken standard lamp has their dressing gowns hanging from it, their scarves wrapped around it, and their slippers knelt against it. The photos of him and his friends now look curiously out at photos of them and their friends staring defiantly back. The clothes he left in his drawers have been wrapped in binbags and pushed to the back. In the bathroom, well, from hotels to childhood homes, all bathrooms look the same. But in case he should ever choose to return to exorcise himself, every bin-bag, ornament and photo has a note at its base detailing where it should be.

Is it worth describing Jack, Jane and Mr Jacobs? Tell someone something, and they either don't picture anything, or as soon as something rings a bell, they wheel in wholesale whatever they've already seen that has that quality. For Jack, Jane's short uncle will forever have his bulbous red nose poking out of eighteenth-century

French military uniform, the spectre of his favourite Hawaiian shirt floating incongruously nearby.

So for what it's worth: Jack has brown hair, Jane blonde and Mr Jacobs grey. They wear different clothes according to the occasion – for instance, at the moment Jack and Jane are in bed, so Jack is wearing boxer shorts and Jane blue (and frilly) pyjamas; no one knows where Mr Jacobs is, he might or might not be in bed. Jack, Jane and Mr Jacobs are not black. This might at first seem a strange announcement, but white is a colour that no one ever seems bothered to mention. If it's of interest, Mr Jacobs' father was born in the Ukraine. Mr Jacobs is half Ukrainian – although he's managed to survive all of his sixty-odd years without a single person asking him 'where are you from?'

Opposite the two wardrobes, between the two bedside tables, on the bed in the middle of the room, Jack and Jane lay asleep. There was knocking on the door, and it was this that woke Jack up. He wondered whether to answer it. Since doors speak but never listen, Jack realised reluctantly that answering the door would involve leaving his bed. He turned to Jane's clammy sleeping body, which lay next to him with width and depth and length. Resting a hand on his bedside table, he turned to the window behind him to confront the stare of the birds in the tree. Still they did nothing.

He turned to look at a back that could be any back, but was the back of the body that he knew Jane ticked and whirred inside. Sometimes he wondered what face he would find on the other side. Feeling it would break the spell, he kissed her neck gently. He said: 'I love you.' The words seemed to rattle limply, so he shifted to see her whole body again, and said again: 'I love you.' It sounded better. It sounded good enough for now. Her body rolled over to face him. Her face shocked him. It was calmly vague in his mind's eye, but when he saw it head-on it was so unchangeably there. He leaned in closer and kissed her lips. They were dry and he pictured the cracked rivets, the dried-glue flakes. 'Morning,' he said, rolling back on to his side and pulling her arm around him medicinally. He spoke out into the room, feeling her breath.

'You've got to remember to book the doctors today.'

'Yes,' said Jack.

'You've got to sort it out.'

'Yes,' said Jack.

'How does your arm feel today? Can you straighten it?'

For some time now Jack's limbs have been slowly seizing up, as if the clockwork was slowly ticking out of them. Jack tries not to think about it, so there's an irony in the fact that you now do. The thing is, nothing is ever perfect anyway. His body felt creaky and painful in the morning, but when you start setting that against amputees and cancer sufferers, it seems a bit silly to pay it much attention. Jane's point was that amputees and cancer sufferers tend to address their problem; maybe if Jack were to do something, then not only would he have a complete set of non-cancerous limbs, but also a complete set of fully functioning ones. Jack's point, well, Jack's point varied and was always sort of vague, but the upshot was that he would sort it out soon. There were only a few things he could no longer do. He couldn't run, lift anything heavy, walk for longer than half an hour or so, and, as of yesterday, pick up a glass of water when he was lying down – after a few seconds' anxiety Jack stumbled across the solution of simply sitting up. The problem, or the solution depending on how you came at it, was how enjoyable were those things anyway? How necessary? He couldn't play the piano, dance the foxtrot or programme a computer. The way Jack saw it, it was simply a case of downsizing. It was efficiency. There was no risk of Jack spreading himself too thinly. Jack was a lump of butter squatting stubbornly in the microwave.

The problem was that the list of actions that were off limits was steadily growing. This is where Jane's point of view comes into its own. Whether he could live a fulfilled and happy life having to sit up every time he wanted a glass of water, was one thing. Whether he could lead a happy and fulfilled life without being able to sit up at all (with or without the belligerent cat-callings of a glass of water) was quite another.

As yet unconsidered in the ongoing debate, is whether Jane can live a happy and fulfilled life constantly discussing the limitations on Jack's. In fact, the more she does discuss it, the less she is sure whether it's concern or annoyance that makes her do so. Every few months there's a night of terrible panic where the whole world holds its breath, as Jack realises his limbs are slowly coming to a standstill. His face drains, his eyes dart erratically, and he pleads with her to tell him that it will be all right, that if he goes to the doctor tomorrow he can get them fixed. And as candles are lit in hospices across the land, as the starving children of Africa solemnly bow their heads, as martyrs and saints sing his prayers, Jack bravely promises to sort it out – if only he could be given another chance. And she holds him, she comforts him, she tells him it will be all right. But then the next day, as wax is being scraped off hospice floors, as children stop looking at their feet and start looking for food, as angels start getting in some quick harp practice, Jack realises that he's bought himself some more time. And Jane uses the time that her boyfriend's acquired, to play with the idea that maybe it's neither annoyance nor concern that make her petition him like this – why the others bother to hold vigil over him is their concern. Maybe it's just that it seems more of an effort not to. She feels more and more as if they both sit idly by, as words that have hatched in their stomachs during the night jostle and flutter their way out of their mouths at day-break.

Jack straightened his arm as far as it would go and then, to show her there was still life in the old dog, ran his hand along her leg.

'That tickles,' she said, and laughed.

Taking the hand and putting it to her face she said: 'I love you.'

He stroked her again and she was unsure whether or not to giggle again.

Jane placed his hand on her right breast, then she placed his hand on her left breast. She held his hand and said: 'Maybe later.'

She kissed his hand, then turned back to go to sleep.

Looking at her, Jack noticed she had a palm-sized patch of chalky dry skin on her shin. He shifted back, thinking of all the flakes that could have nestled into him during the night.

'Would you love me if I didn't have a nose?' he asked absent-mindedly.

'Yes,' was the reply that crawled across the contours of the pillow.

'Really?'

'Well, you'd have a metal nose or something. You couldn't just have a hole there. So yes, I reckon I could live with a metal nose.'

'Well, what if we didn't have enough money for a metal nose, so I had to go with glass and you could see right in?'

'Yes.'

'Bees?'

'What?'

'A nose made of bees. Genetically modified ones that buzzed in formation and I could smell through them. If I lost my nose, and I had a choice between a metal nose that covered it up, or a specially developed artificial nose that gave me back my sense of smell, but the side effect was that this special nose was made of bees. Would you let me have the bee nose, or would you say I could either give up smell or give up you?'

'You could have the bee nose.'

'Wasps?'

'What?' Jane continued to exhale after the word to indicate gently the theme of sleep.

'What if the nose was made of wasps?'

'Anything, I don't care.'

'What if I couldn't find a donor and the only way I could get my new nose was for them to first grow the wasp nose on you?'

'Oh just shut up, Jack. You're not being funny.'

He stared at her shin again.

'It is difficult for me to believe that you would stand by me if I had an insect nose, when you can't even find it in you to discuss the various alternatives.'

Turning away from the scaly patch of skin, Jack looked out of the window behind him. Outside a breeze carried the branches up and down and so too went the birds, up and down, up and down. The birds didn't seem aware of their movement, though; they sat calmly and stared blankly as if it were the trunk of the tree that was falling down and up, down and up around them. Their expression reminded him of birds that sat on the sea, floating back and forth with the waves. Jack reached up and pushed the window further open – he did this with ease, a glass of water might have the dexterity to outfox him, but a window is a flat-footed foe. He could faintly hear their singing, but their eyes were blank: the eyeballs mushy, crushable, disconnected. The birds' aurora of sound continued to flicker like some broken language, all half-words and conjunctions. He wondered what transmitted the sound that these funny creatures were catching snippets of like broken radios.

Jack closed the window and clapped his hands together, in the way someone does when everyone's been sat around for a while. He turned back to Jane and said brightly: 'We've woken up early.'

She turned around sleepily and he pushed a smile up on her face. His thumb caught her and she winced briefly. There's always something, he thought, annoyed. He waited and saw that she held the smile there, so he said: 'Shall we call someone before they go to work?'

Jane looked at him blankly and then checked herself. 'Yeah, why not?'

'Who shall we call?'

She thought. She tried hard to think of someone because it might be fun; it should be fun. 'I don't know,' she said. 'Whoever,' she added, hopefully.

'It would just be funny, no one would ever expect us to be up this early, we can both speak to them and let them know we're up.' He flicked through the numbers on his phone.

'Everyone will still be asleep, though,' Jane said.

She got up and walked across the room. He was about to tell her about the dry skin when she handed him the camera and laughed: 'Take a photo, you can do it in the mirror and then we can post it to people to prove we were awake.'

He kissed her and stroked her legs as she climbed back into bed, carefully pulling the cover up over her. She lay down on his chest as he angled the camera. 'Remember to get the clock in,' she said, 'otherwise we could have taken it at any time.'

He angled the camera so the clock was in shot.

'Have you got everything in?'

'If I include the clock then you lose the bed sheets.'

'Just take it, silly. I can't believe we're doing this anyway, who'll want to see the photo anyway.'

'When does anyone ever want to see photos?' Jack put the camera down, breathed in deeply and stretched.

Jane stroked his chest and said: 'People say that the guy wants to go nearest the door because it's like the cave door.'

'I think I'm just here because you wanted that side, aren't I?' Jack smiled. 'It's all silly.'

She wrapped her leg over him. He put his arm around her. She put her head on his chest. They kissed. Then as she rolled back to go to sleep, Jack heard the knocking at the door again and wondered who it might be. He got out of bed and walked to the bathroom.

Sitting on the toilet he pushed his head against the window trying to see who it was. Jack had a theory. Well, Jack had many theories, but this one was particularly pertinent now. The pertinent theory was this: if you told yourself that the worst possible scenario was going to come true, then it wouldn't. It is of course a vague theory and not one he espoused at dinner parties – largely because he was never invited to them – but it hinged on a feeling he had, that the purpose of bad things happening, was how terrible they made you feel. If you doubt it, think of a better reason for them. Now here was the deal, if you worried about the bad thing before it happened, then you'd paid your debt to it, so having got its dues why would it bother to go through the motions? It wouldn't: that's the gem of it. Jack let the panic of it being Mr Jacobs at the door wash through him. Yesterday, Mr Jacobs had, for the first time in about a year, turned up at the house when Jane had failed to exchange a pair of vitally important black-ribbed socks for a now obsolete book on English landscaping: *1920 to the present day*. On finding his house empty of Jane he had quickly made his excuses and left, but not before quickly jotting down a note and handing it sternly to Jack. It had said: 'Dearest Janey, Why have you ruined my house? I left it in your care. Jay.' The worst possible scenario was that Mr Jacobs would find his house still ruined: Jack's stomach sank.

The knocking stopped and Jack smiled. If he ever did get invited to a dinner party, then he just so happened to have a little theory that would pretty much guarantee him getting invited back. This satisfaction was immediately replaced by the unsettling realisation that, despite the absence of Jane, Mr Jacobs had still braved the bathroom. Where his bottom was, was where Mr Jacobs' bottom had been only a day before. Mr Jacobs had put the suitcase down, Jack had picked it up. Had Jane used it since or had she gone at work? It wasn't the sort of thing to bother her, which seemed bizarre for someone who so fastidiously washed her hands before eating. And she liked toilet books as well; a grubby chain letter passed from sitter to sitter. He carefully peeled off a piece of toilet paper, and used it to guard his fingers against the inner tube. Although, he thought, letting objectivity have a quick run around, his skin didn't swallow things; it was really more like a glove. He held on to this thought as he washed his hands quickly and left. The Bad Thing had realised he'd faked the worry and exacted its payment by other means.

Trying not to wake Jane up, he climbed quietly back into bed. Then suddenly there was the steady crashing of feet up the stairs. He wondered if the front door had grown so tired of being knocked on, that it had used some initiative and answered itself. The bedroom door crashed open and a voice leapt excitedly through it.

'The guy in the newsagents said I sounded as if I was from Birmingham.'

The words hung on John's broad toothy smile like flies stuck to a swatter. It was just broader than a broad smile. If he could have got away with it, John would have put on blue felt tears for when he was sad, and sunshine stickers for when he was happy. The Baptist smile John had stretched as he ran up the stairs, gave way to its own little messiah when he realised he'd managed to interrupt a couple in a private moment and thrown a non-sequitur in their face. No one wants to be a lonely guy in a dead-end job. But if you shove a screen around the guy, if you give him posters and a soundtrack, then suddenly his life doesn't seem so bad. Now the guy can't hear the soundtrack, and he doesn't know about the millions of people who are rooting for him – but imagine how happy he'd be if he did. John's taken this leap of faith, and no matter what's happening to him the audience are on his side. So it wasn't a problem when he quit his career to work part-time in the local newsagents, because it meant he got to spend more time with the girl who worked in the florists next door: it was romantic. For every person who told him it was a mistake, there were thousands who could see it for what it really was.

'But you are from Birmingham,' Jack replied, immediately annoyed with himself: he'd set himself up to be cast by John as the grumpy straight man. The producers returned from their huddle, with the perfect scene plotted out: John was the loveable moron with no idea of etiquette, Jack the put-upon friend.

John smiled. Jack glared.

Jack said: 'You know, if there's one good thing about delusion, it's surely the free rein it gives you. You'd think you'd try to be a bit more glamorous. Even if you weren't from the Midlands, for love of God live a little, try somewhere abroad.'

John smiled. Jack glared.

Jack said: 'But there we are, if there's a second good thing about delusion, it's that it can at least boast self-determinism.'

John smiled. But before Jack could glare, John's eyes whipped his head towards the window. His eyebrows leapt up his forehead, as if trying to join his head-hair's cosy Emperor Penguin huddle; the skin around his eyes stretched open in budding bloom. This is the wonder of the close-up, you see, you'd miss it all if you saw John at the theatre.

John looked imploringly at Jack, then stared meaningfully out of the window, flickering thoughts through his eyes like a slideshow of holiday snaps. Jack wonders whether John can see the birds. Jack wonders whether the birds can see him. Every muscle in John's body contracted to see which one could crouch smallest. His head moved with slow, eager concentration from left to right, like a dog tracking food being passed around a table. Jack looked jealously at Jane, who was managing to sleep through all of this. He pulled the covers up, reasoning that he could at least pretend to.

When Jack was sure the pretty girl had left the frame of the window, he sat up again. Guilty at having been caught 'lost in the moment', John slid his eyes from side to side, like a ventriloquist's dummy that'd been told he had to go back in the box.

John's phone began to ring. Holding it at arm's distance as if it was a bomb, John said: 'What do I say?'

'Say hello,' Jack said. 'Or tell them you're from Birmingham.'

'You can't joke about this, it's Jenny.'

'Jenny, your girlfriend?'

'Yes.'

'Jenny, your girlfriend who you live with?'

'Yes.'

'Well, you're ahead on this one because she already knows where you grew up. Just say hello and wing it from there.'

'That's typical of you. All wry and insensitive. Stuff like this never bothers you.'

'What stuff? There is no stuff yet. Your girlfriend, who you live with, is ringing you. Presumably you've spoken to her before. You're forgetting I've seen her, her conversation must be something pretty special.'

'No, you see I just ran out of the house without telling her. I just had to get out. And now she knows I've gone. She knows I just left her all by herself. I just had to tell you something. Something beautiful.'

'Say you popped over to say hello to your friend. I think it's a lie you may just be able to pull off.'

'I can't, I can't. Then she'll be all: "Well, why didn't you tell me" and "Why didn't you want to be with me" and "Well, I might have wanted something from the shop." Help me, think of something. I mean she might have wanted me to pick up some food. A good boyfriend would be bringing her back roses and cooking breakfast in bed, and I'm not even thinking whether she needs me to buy her a snack from the shop.'

John's big on all that malarkey, and at first glance you might mistake him for a romantic. Breakfast in bed is better than break-fast at a table; laying your coat down over a puddle is better than walking around the puddle; the first kiss with the girl of your dreams is better when she has a boyfriend, or you have a girlfriend, or your families are at war and it'll lead to your early deaths. John would upset whoever happened to be the current love of his life, simply for the chance to stand for days on end in the pouring rain till she took him back.

Oddly though, this orienteering through the checkpoints of romance hasn't affected the clothes he wears. Jack often wonders why John doesn't get all dressed up; given his frequent visits to the land of love, you'd have thought he'd have bothered to buy the T-shirt. Preppy romantic hero clothes maybe, or perhaps a sharp suit set off by a trilby, neatly groomed moustache and a rose in the lapel. Or, given recent developments, a Blues shirt so people would know he was a City fan. But to John, clothes are as soullessly func-tional as toilets, staff Christmas parties and the little sip of wine a person takes before it is served. There's a certain kind of person that dresses like a hippy in advertising campaigns: clothes that look cobbled together, but cobbled nonetheless by a master cobbler. John is to Gap Menswear what a crack whore is to heroin chic: the real deal. A pure blood. He wears something chest-shaped on his chest, something legs-shaped on his legs and then finally for equally practical reasons: shoes – which are of course foot-shaped.

Maybe John hasn't thought it through that well. Jack doesn't know, because he can't think of a way to bring it up with him, without sounding as if he's unpicking the stitches of his friend for fun. But if Jack had to guess he'd say that clothes were too obvious. He'd say that, ironic as it sounds, it would make John feel false. As much of an act as it seems, that's not what he wants. So Jack's guess would be – and it is just a guess – that John's dressing in no particular way at all lets people get right through to him. And then what they see – or being cynical about his motives, what they think they see – is the real thing. And no matter how untrue you know the words are when they're squatting rigid in your head, it's hard to ignore the show they make in the lines of someone else's face. So maybe, Jack guesses – and it is just a guess – maybe John's not so much crazy as extreme, not so much extreme as uncomplicated. That's what Jack would say if he had to guess, which thankfully he doesn't.

The phone kept ringing. John kept staring at it. John kept trying to pull Jack into the tension.

Then out of nowhere John said: 'What happened to Jane's legs?'

'I don't know. It's kind of weird. Look, just answer the phone.'

Jack moved the duvet to cover her. The patch seemed to have grown slightly, and there seemed to be a bit he hadn't noticed before on the other leg.

Whitewashing everything that'd been said before, John said: 'I have to, I have to answer it.'

He stares at Jack intently as if it's just the way things have got to be, he's got to take that bullet, he's got to answer the damn phone.

'Hang in there, tiger, I got your back covered,' Jack replies.

John answered the phone.

'Hello, honey,' he said in a voice weary of its guilt. 'Where am I? I . . .' He looked wildly around him. 'I am . . .'

'You are at your friend's house. You are in the house across the road. You are thirty metres away.'

Jack spoke in that strange neutral voice people get when they're anything but neutral, the one that suggests that every ounce of strength they have is going into controlling their frustration; leaving their face dead like a mask and their voice drained and transparent.

'I just had to get out of the house. Look, there's nothing in it. I'm sorry, I just popped out to get a paper. Honestly. I'm not meeting up with a girl or anything.'

If there's a sun in the sky and grass on the land, she won't have said anything about him meeting up with any girls. And there is a sun in the sky, albeit a sallow orange one, and there is grass on the land, albeit patchy and strangely brown, and Jenny definitely hadn't mentioned girls up to this point. Jack couldn't hear her, but he had a feeling she might be mentioning girls now. He could hear her voice scratching its way out of the phone. John held it at arm's distance again, and looked around frantically as if there was no way to stop the chain of events now in place.

'You've got to do this for me,' he told Jack desperately, pleadingly, and then said to the phone: 'Jack told me to come over, I've got responsibilities to him too.'

At this he promptly hung up.

Jack stared at him. His head quivered from side to side, his eyebrows wriggled as far down as their roots would allow, and his lips pursed and relaxed as they tried to say: why? Of course, this isn't because he'd lost the ability to actually speak the word 'why'. What had happened was infuriating, but it hadn't brought on a stroke; he's not that delicate. But saying 'why' once wouldn't do the same justice to his incredulity as the army of a thousand phantom smoke-ringed whys that were now flying in all directions at John.

John looked at Jack, defeated.

'I'm sorry, but I can't have her getting upset right now. It would be selfish of me to let her get upset.'

What on earth would you say to this? Jack couldn't think of anything.

Pleased at this, John continued: 'I can't. I couldn't. You don't understand. You could never understand.'

The grin had gone now. For a moment Jack wondered whether he was genuinely upset.

'I wish . . . I wish you could know, you would see then.'

'See what? I thought you came over here to tell me about something beautiful.'

'I can't . . . It's Jenny, sort of. Jenny's changed. It started happening a while ago, but today when I woke up, and she was still asleep, I looked at her, and I saw it properly for the first time. And she'll have woken up and had to see it on her own. I'm just so selfish, I just thought about how it made me feel, and how I wanted to share that with someone, and I didn't once think about her having to deal with it on her own. But it's beautiful, Jack, I just hope she can see that. What's happened is just so beautiful.'

Determined not to ask what in the name of sweet Jesus John was talking about, Jack focused on making sure his face didn't attempt to ask behind his back.

'There's nothing I can do now. I was hoping to talk to you quickly, but she'll have noticed I've gone by now. However quick I rush back, whatever excuses I give her, all she'll say is: "But you left the house without telling me." I've blown it, Jack. I had it all and I think this time I might have blown it.'

John looked down at the floor and then stared at Jack. Jack watched him stare down at the floor and then stared back. Like two Pavlovian dogs, their minds both salivate the words that conclude one of John's dramas. Consequently they don't bother to say them, but for some reason still pause for the amount of time it would have taken them to. John felt a wave of frustration lashing against him, as Jack didn't say: 'What is the point in all this?'

The phantom of an imploring face shimmered in front of Jack, as John didn't reply: 'But you don't understand, you can't see what's really going on.'

John let 'I'd better be going back' slip resignedly out of the corner of his mouth.

As he turned to go, Jack noticed that John was still wearing his slippers. While his mind wondered whether the incongruous footwear was planned or not, his mouth leapt at the window of opportunity and asked: 'What is it? What's beautiful?'

John turned his head, a low-headed, shoulder-hunched Eeyore twist, you could almost see the ears flop down weakly.

'I'm sorry. I was wrong for dragging you into it. I wanted to tell you but I can't. Believe me, I wish there was another way. But she can't know I just went out of my own accord without telling her. She can't know that. I can't go into it but she's vulnerable right now. Delicate. And she needs me. I should be with her all the time.'

'But why? Why can't she know her boyfriend's across the street on his own steam?'

Jack mimes pulling on the rope of an old-fashioned train-whistle to try and lighten the mood. He caricatures his face so John knows he's being flippant. There's nothing worse than people not knowing you're being ironic.

John's lips found the strength to muster a thin smile. Tired by this gesture, they squeezed out: 'Because I shouldn't be. I shouldn't be here, I should be there with her. She needs me.'

'Is she ill?'

Jack couldn't hear any note of concern in his voice when he said this, because admittedly there was not even a crotchet of concern there. Jack is not a witch doctor, and has never found his ill wishes affect those around him. Happily, this gives him carte blanche to imagine all kinds of terrible things and get the satisfaction of them coming true, with none of the responsibility. In this case, though, he wishes nothing bad on Jenny, at least until he can see for himself what it is that's so beautiful. It's just that when things are serious, he always gets in a terrible panic that people might think he's being insincere. And so, anything he says to suggest he does care is filtered through this self-conscious sieve. Every syllable churned around by little bristly hands clawing: 'Show you care, show you care, show you care.' So the end product always sounds clinical, the sound of detergent. A steel white angular effect, which he sits desperately behind, trying to soften out the edges with a tilting head and widening eyes.

Jack said it again, but mixes the words up a bit to see if that helps: 'She's not ill, is she?'

'No. No, it's beautiful. If only I could tell you. God, if only I could tell the world how beautiful it is. But it's our thing, you see. And, well, it means she needs me. And I'm such a selfish bastard that I ignore that and carry on doing what the hell I like. I really don't deserve her. She puts up with so much from me.'

Feeling as though he was constructing the words from an Ikea furniture manual, Jack said: 'Well, I'm glad to hear she's OK.'

To show his gratitude John started rhythmically nodding. Speaking slowly and carefully, because he wanted to make sure it got through to him, Jack carefully putted his words under the falling head: 'And if she's up to it and it doesn't shatter the crystalline beauty you're both hiding in there, maybe you could tell her I had nothing to do with it?'

'I'll try,' John said earnestly, and for a moment Jack felt grateful. 'If I think I can get away with it I'll try.'

And with this he slowly slunk out of the room, his slippers dragging reluctantly along the floor. As he reached the door he turned and, looking down at his fidgeting hands, he said: 'I couldn't stop you following me. If you followed me and climbed in by the open lounge window, that really wouldn't be my fault.'

Then his voice did one of those disconcerting switches, when it stops sliding and snaps into a different key. Each word shot out with a sharp crisp certainty.

'I know you think I'm melodramatic, Jack. But this is different. It's a strange thing that's happened, but it is beautiful. We've got to keep it a secret because God knows how people would react. But it is beautiful, Jack. And you really have no way of knowing till you've seen her.'

He set his eyes firmly on Jack.

'Follow me,' he said.

And then turned and left.

Slightly taken aback by John's closing words, Jack nudged Jane to try and wake her up. He imagined John striding purposefully back to his house and suddenly felt strangely belittled. He nudged Jane a little harder.

'I do love you, honey,' he whispered in her ear.

He knew when he told Jane she would laugh at the idea of John having some terrible secret he had to cope with bravely. But there'd been a look of conviction in his eyes, a sense of control, which made Jack feel as if his friend had been tolerating his teasing and condescension, rather than suffering it. He hugged himself closer to Jane.

'Come on, honey, wake up. If you wake up now I'll make you breakfast in bed.'

Jack pulled the covers down to wake her, but as he did he saw that the patch of dry skin had spread to cover both legs. Only her toes peeked curiously out at the ends. Jack leapt backwards, steadying himself on the windowsill. Her legs were now completely chainmailed in little fingernail-sized plates of hardened curls. At her hip, where it had only just begun to take hold, it was a chalky, dusty white. Down by her ankle, shards of brittle black skin knifed up in every direction.

'Jane,' he said weakly, hearing his voice tiptoe around the room. 'Jane, wake up.'

He yanked at the duvet cover, but it brushed against the top of her leg and the soft chalky flakes billowed and danced in a cloud around her. Pulling gently now, he dragged the rest of the cover off slowly. He heard a tear as it caught on the spikes at the bottom of her legs.

'Jane, I think you've hurt your leg,' he called to her, feeling at once scared and ridiculous.

He looked down and stared at the toes, which after a while, poking out of the leathered scales, looked now like strange growths. After a few minutes of staring hypnotised at the strange toes, he realised he should be doing something. He called to her again but she wouldn't wake. He braced himself to reach over and shake her but couldn't force himself to move. His hand grabbed at a book from his bedside table. When he realised what he was about to do, he tried to make the throw as gentle as possible. It landed heavily on her face and slid down to rest in the gully of her neck.

Jane didn't move. There seemed something disrespectful in leaving the book sticking into her like this, so he tentatively reached over to knock it away. As he leant in closer he noticed that the chalky white curls had already hardened into dark brown crisps. Her stomach was now flaking and cracking. It looked like the speeded up shots of decay in documentaries, the drying cracking skin creeping resolutely up her body.

It climbed up and under the arch of her chin and clambered up around her mouth. Her lips quivered and then sealed. It curved up like a river and sank down into her sockets. The hair on her head fizzled as it washed over it and then she was gone. Jack stood back numbly and stared in horror at the cocoon.

If a bystander were put into this scene, he would – after getting over the initial shock of being transported into a room in order simply to stand by – be surprised by two things. The first thing that would have surprised the bystander, but is by now old hat to everyone else, is that Jane has been cocooned in her own dead skin. Shocking as this is, the bystander might consider this appropriate compensation for his troubles. Being stripped of every last inch of your personality, and shoved into the hollow clothes of a neutral observer, cannot be a wholly pleasant experience. But if it has to happen, then you'd hope it was at least to be witness to something noteworthy. Given you've lost the experiences of a lifetime, it would be nice to have something dramatic enough to trigger a new appreciation of the world – although what kind of personality would be created with this sight as its foundation stone is debatable.

While coming to terms with this, the bystander would then have been hit by his second surprise. And while not being as visually dramatic as the first, it is just as disturbing. The second thing that would surprise the man being born in the corner of the room would be the complete lack of surprise now present in Jack's face, and, by implication, the lack of surprise in his head. What would raise the eyebrows of the man standing just out of the action but just in shot would be the sleepiness in Jack's own eyebrows; they, that is, the two eyebrows, that is, the two pairs of eyebrows, would contrast each other well; which is worth looking out for if contrast pleases you – which it should. What on earth the bystander would do at this point would be interesting to speculate on. But then as soon as he started doing anything, he would, by definition, cease to be a bystander, and so by the rules of his incorporation, cease to exist; disappearing as he stepped over the boundaries of his life's lot. But then the bystander never existed in the first place – which is better or worse for him depending on what you judge important.

Just because there was no bystander doesn't mean that Jack hadn't become surprisingly unsurprised. Because he had – squirrels are well aware of trees falling in their forests and are often woken up by them. But if the bystander also happened to be a shadowy figure from Jack's past, and if he had a friend with him or happened to be the sort of shadowy figure that quite liked talking aloud to himself, he might have been moved to say: 'Ahh, he must have remembered now, it must all be coming back to him. All this has happened before, a long, long time ago.' Due to the mundane setting of a suburban bedroom, and to the determination of a 100-watt bulb to eliminate any shadows one might choose to lurk in, no shadowy figure bothered to make an entrance. It might be hoped that Jack would have said something to clarify the subject, but given the shock of what had just happened, and the fact that there was now no one left to hear him speak, it is perhaps understandable that he remained silent. He did think something, though. But with no one there to question him, why he thought it remains uncertain. What Jack thought, through the hazy concoction of shock and surfacing repressed memories, his eyes staring fixedly at the birds in the tree outside, was: Why would John think this is beautiful?

Nina-Marie Gardner

Nina-Marie Gardner was born in New York City and received a BA in English from Yale University. *I'm Not This Girl* is her first novel. She currently lives in London with her dog and is also working on a play and a collection of short stories.

I'm Not This Girl

I was standing on the corner of Broadway and Spring Street, waiting for my friend Jules, feeling the sort of emptiness a girl feels when there's no boy on the horizon and everything slows down 'til it seems as simple and silent as a whisper.

The best part about being alone was the way my life started to feel like my own little secret.

I'd been waiting for awhile but it wasn't Jules' fault; I was early. And just when I was starting to feel weird and paranoid and self-conscious, I saw Jules on the other side of Broadway.

Yo Pippi!, I hollered. Jules had red hair and freckles so of course I called her *Pippi*.

I watched her cross the street, darting in front of a speeding cab as fast as a minnow.

The thing about Jules was that she was the only girl I'd ever met who was smarter and had done more drugs than me. From the moment we met we both agreed that there was something *fierce* about two small girls hanging out.

Hey, Freak. What's shakin?, she said, giving me a quick hug and a kiss on the cheek. Where's your dog?

In Montauk. The little shit.

Damn. I wanna be your dog.

No kidding. So what's up? Are you hungry? Where should we go?

I don't know. I kinda feel like a Margarita.

Oh God, I'm not supposed to drink, I said.

Oh. Right. The intervention. I forgot.

A week earlier I'd been ambushed by what I liked to refer to as *The Botched Intervention Attempt*. My boss invited me to lunch and after a bottle of wine she got all teary-eyed and said I had a serious drug problem. Apparently she wore my coat to lunch a few weeks ago after mistaking it for her own and found an empty vial of cocaine in the pocket, which she thought was crack.

Why did they think it was crack? Jules asked when I told her about it.

The vial I guess, I told her, and we had a good laugh about it, although in reality the situation was pretty grim. Basically now everyone in my office thought I was a crack head. And to make matters worse, I didn't even get fired.

So, Jules said, you wanna just go get a coffee or something?

I wasn't prepared for how much it hurt to witness Jules trying to stoop to the whole sober coffee routine, just for my sake.

Jules. I want. A fucking. DRINK. We're going to Jones. They've got great Margaritas.

Oooh! I love Jones . . . But . . .

What?

Are you sure? I don't want to get you in trouble . . .

Yea. Right, I said. Shut the fuck up. Of course you want to get me in trouble. Thank God — at least I have someone who's not trying to *help* me.

Fuck that.

Right?

Who helps people?

Jesus. I know. What's the point?

I'd *much* rather get into trouble.

Word.

Troublemaker.

Aw shucks.

So, do they take credit cards?

I fuckin' hope so – I don't have any cash.

Yo, me neither.

Cool. So let's go.

Cool.

And we smiled at each other as I lit up a cigarette which we shared as we walked up Broadway towards Great Jones Street.

Jules and I first met at this weekly loft party on Walker Street that I used to go to on Wednesdays. The guy who threw the party was this speed freak who was trying to turn the loft where he lived into some kind of Warhol Factory art gallery party scene – or something. No one really cared what the guy's deal was, but it was a fucking awesome party. I missed pretty much every Thursday at work because of it.

One night in the early days of this party I was tripping on some pure MDMA that I'd snorted, sorta getting horny and looking around for potential cute boys to drag home and go to bed with, when I noticed this girl. She was staring at me – staring and smiling – and I was impressed 'cause her pupils looked like they were probably bigger than mine.

Rolling or stoned? she said, and of course I liked her immediately.

Rolling, I said. And stoned.

We both laughed.

Me too, she said.

I could see my ex-boyfriend Laurent talking to this nasty-looking French chick who'd been following him around all night. Word on the street was that he was crashing with her.

Never takes him long, I thought.

I was having a hard time picturing them in bed together, though overall I'd been doing pretty well since we'd split up. But it was hard always seeing him at parties. We hadn't quite moved past the phase where we'd pretend not to notice each other but by the end of the night we'd be out on some stairwell fucking each other's brains out. Since we broke up, our sex life had never been better.

What are you looking at? Jules asked me.

My ex, I told her, nodding towards Laurent.

Which one? The one who keeps moving around like he can't stand still? With the goatee?

Yea.

Neither of us said anything for a moment. I was starting to get the spins and must have made some sort of groan, because Jules said something like, That's hot.

I felt suddenly and completely embarrassed and I wished desperately that I had another pill.

Huh? I said. I knew what she'd said.

You're hot, she said.

What? I said. No matter how many drugs I did, I couldn't handle compliments. They made me feel like a slug turned inside-out after it's been dropped in a puddle of beer.

You moaned. I can tell you're the kind of person who makes noises – even when you think. I'll bet you make a lot of sounds in the shower.

Oh . . . my God. I wasn't sure what to say. How did you know . . .?

I can just tell. I'm talented like that – haha. So, what's up with *her*?

That girl he's talking to? With the hair? I dunno. I guess he's fucking her.

The French chick? With the big ass?

Yea!

No! That girl he's talking to?

Yes.

Oh God, I'm sorry if this is raw for you – but ugh, man! She's a bitch.

You know her?

No. Do you?

No.

But she's a bitch, said Jules.

Huh.

Look at her ass!

Yea. It's big.

So?

So . . .?

So . . . How can she be so snotty with an ass like that?

Oh Lord. I'm not even gonna go *near* that one.

What? Her butt? said Jules.

NO!! What you just said . . . Jeesh. Never mind. Continue. This is good.

Well, said Jules, I know for a fact she's mean. I mean, she doesn't talk to girls.

Maybe she doesn't speak English.

Yea but . . . She still talks to boys.

Hmmm. You're right.

He's hot, said Jules, staring at Laurent. He's really fucking hot.

Yea. I know.

Is he gay?

I don't know. Probably.

When did you guys break up?

About a month ago.

Bummer.

Yea.

But you're too good for him.

Yea.

Definitely.

Yea, but . . . it sucks.

I know.

Guys suck.

Word. *Girls*, on the other hand . . .

If only I was gay.

I am.

What? Oh . . . oh. You're into girls?

Jules nodded. Sometimes guys, she said, mostly girls.

I guess I'm into mostly guys.

Too bad, she said. But the way we were smiling at each other I don't think either one of us was feeling anything but completely turned on.

I forgot all about Laurent that night and spent the whole night talking and flirting with Jules. We never kissed or hooked up, but from that night onwards we became the best of friends.

We shared our life stories, and vented, and flirted, and drank heavily, and smoked pot, and took ecstasy, and did coke. We enjoyed one another's company in that special, mutually supportive way shared exclusively by those who are dedicated to the reckless and forbidden pleasure of getting completely fucked up.

We grabbed a wobbly corner table at Jones, our favorite greasy Cajun café, which had pretty bad food but was cheap and had the best Bloody Marys and Margaritas in all of Manhattan.

Every time I go to Jones I think about New Orleans, I hate that place, I said.

Watch out sister, said Jules. Look where you are. Plus you know it's very uncool not to like New Orleans.

Good.

I've never been.

Don't go. It's disgusting.

What's wrong with it?

It's just – it's gross. Too much drinking.

So far so good.

I had my first and only Long Island Iced Tea there – got so fucked up next thing I knew I was making out with some sailor.

So?

Jules!!!! A SAILOR!! Like, in a UNIFORM! How crazy is that! A fucking SAILOR!

Wow. A sailor. Gosh. Should we get something to eat?

I guess so. You hungry?

No. Are you?

No. But we should get something.

What are crawfish?

Ugh. They're gross. Let's get them.

Trouble?

Trouble with a large pitcher of Margaritas.

Awesome.

I can't believe I have to go to work tomorrow.

You still have that job?

Yea, well, I'm leaving after this month.

I was gonna say – the crack, right?

Coke. Whatever. Same difference.

So you're still working there? That must be weird.

Um, *Yea*. 'Cause they all think I'm on crack.

The waitress brought the crawfish and Margaritas, and for some reason the crawfish seemed really bug-like.

Jules, I whispered, they look like spiders!

Oh my God! Shhhhh, she giggled.

I can't even look at them!

Shhh! Have a Margarita – Jules poured me a Margarita and in no time both of us had forgotten all about the creepy crawly crawfish.

After four pitchers of Margaritas at Jones I couldn't turn down Jules' invitation to extend our evening together by grabbing a drink with her someplace else. We went to Barramundi on Ludlow, which I loved, because a guy once told me he loved me there and they were cool about me bringing my dog.

Jules and I snuggled into a corner banquette and began slugging down Caipirinhas, something I needed like I needed a bullet in my head. I was feeling great.

Have an affair with me, said Jules.

Shit girl, beat around the bush why don't you? Oh wait –

I want you.

Jules!

C'mon!

Kiss me!

And I paused for a second, and thought about it, and then I just figured, why not? Considering all the drinks in my bloodstream I was fueled up for just about anything.

So there we were, no big deal, the kind of thing that goes on all the time in bars all over the Lower East Side of New York – just two little girls making out in a booth.

And as we kissed I thought, Wow – Jules is right – kissing girls is pretty damn nice!

Suddenly we noticed the bartender bringing us this enormous tray of drinks – at least half the guys in the place had decided to buy us a round of drinks.

The second we'd walked into the bar that night, however, I'd spied a beautiful boy by the bar. He was the pretty, lanky, boyish type I tend to go nuts for. So every now and again, between drinks and kissing Jules, I kept sneaking peeks at the bar to make sure he was still there.

God, I thought, every time I looked over at him, God, he's *so hot*.

He was cute in the way I thought Luke Skywalker was cute when I was fourteen. I was pretty sure he knew I was watching him, and he seemed to like it, but just as I was about to break it to Jules that I was after him, I saw him walk by in the reflection of the mirror. I turned and he was out the front door.

It was all I could do to keep from howling right there at the table. Instead I just sighed and bravely told myself that I was a big girl who didn't give a shit . . .

But I did hit the speed dial on my cell, figuring as long as the night was going to hell, I might as well call Fred, this record label guy I had amazing sex with but was trying to erase from my life 'cause he was such a slime-bag.

Luckily Jules caught me before the call went through, You were checking that guy out, the one that just left – weren't you? she said. What, did you think he was cute?

Yea. No. Yes. Not really. Kinda. I don't know. Whatever. Who cares? He's just a guy. Fuck it. I'm calling Fred.

I thought you hated Fred! Which one is he again?

I do hate him. The hockey player. Music label guy. Fucking asshole.

Don't do it!! Be strong!

Jules!! But I'm drunk!

So get drunker! So you don't do it!

Waaa. But I wanna. Please Jules? Please? Just tonight?

But Jules shook her head no.

Okay, fine, you're right. I don't want to call him. I feel like shit. I want to go home . . .

And then *Lo and Behold*, who should reenter the bar, but Skywalker himself. He came in with his friend, and they were smiling no less, and heading right towards our table.

Jules! Oh my God!

I know, I know, sit still, here they come!

They must have discussed us after leaving the bar!, I thought — and the fact that they'd decided to come back — well that could only mean one thing . . .!!

Jules! I think this is one of my absolute most favorite moments in life!

Shhhhhh!

No, but Jules — you know what this is, right? This is the moment before. This is that moment when I *know it's going to happen*.

Hey. Can we sit here? And when he sat down beside me it was perfect, and I felt that orange glow at the base of my stomach start to flame. I could barely sit still — my mouth went dry and I licked my lips and started wiggling my feet under the table with glee.

Oh Joy! Oh Bliss!

We were all fairly drunk and everyone knew where the evening was going so conversation was forgettable and sloppy. But my Luke Skywalker was a doll, and his real name was Alex — he said he grew up in New Haven and he played in a band and he was even a substitute teacher! Under the table he held my hand and I felt like I could taste him long before I brought him home.

I woke at 5:45, well before my alarm was set to go off at 6:30. I knew if I moved, my head would start hurting so I just lay there and stared at the digital numbers on my cheap clock radio. I was trying not to think about the beautiful boy who appeared to be naked, asleep in my bed.

When the clock said 6:02 I leaned carefully over, gazing at the curve of his shoulder. I thought of a swan and I wanted to touch all along the edge of his shoulder blade but I knew it would wake him. And in the end the best part of all is when they're still sleeping.

The next time I looked the clock said 6:18 and my breath caught in a spasm of panic. I'd been having this feeling lately, like if I slipped just a little, the world would clang down and crash all over me. My hangover was going to be huge. I pressed my head down on the pillow enjoying the cool surface on my forehead.

I wanted to curl up in a ball beside him, burrow at his side and just hold on to him for a while. I wanted to be pressed hard into something dense and solid and strong. I couldn't keep all my pieces together, and I felt unbalanced, like I'd already lost a few. I needed someone to hold on to a few things while I picked up the stuff that had fallen just out of reach.

I couldn't do it. I couldn't be late. I hated my job and I hated my life but I had to get up.

He opened an eye and then drew me into his arms, and even though I was already panicking and burning with hangover his fingers on my back were the kindest thing anyone had done for me in a long, long time.

Just being touched, I thought, had to be one of the most under-rated ingredients necessary to human survival.

Don't go to work, he said, call in sick – let's just stay in bed together all day.

Who are you? I thought.

Is that a yes?

Oh God, if you only knew . . . I could hardly look at him. I can't be late for work – it's a long story –

He chuckled and squeezed me tighter and I wanted to cry. I weighed the possibilities and looked again at the clock – it now read 6:42.

No. I can't. I really have to go to work. I felt like an ass.

He raised an eyebrow in disbelief and looked at me. He was a sweetheart. I thought I might be sick – which is probably the only reason I was able to leap from the bed towards the bathroom.

When he joined me in the shower I thought I might be hallucinating. Well, if I am tripping, I figured, I definitely have to get a hell of a lot more of whatever it is that I'm on.

I stood and concentrated really hard, ignoring my hangover and trying to take in and remember every little detail of how I felt and what was happening so I'd have it for later.

We said goodbye in front of my building, and even though I knew I was going to be late I let him take his time as he kissed me. I wanted to drag him back into my apartment. But somehow I managed to stay there, kissing on my stoop on Avenue B as schoolchildren straggled by dragging their book bags on tiny luggage trolleys.

It was verging on 7:30. I was going to be really late. I pulled myself away from his kiss.

It's good you came back to the bar last night.

Your friend winked at me.

What!

You didn't know? That's why I came back.

Oh my God.

I didn't want to leave anyway, but I was with my friend.

She winked at you? That's why you came back?

Yea. But I knew – I saw you looking at me.

Oh my God.

We kissed some more. He was a really good kisser.

You're a good kisser, he said. My grip was slipping, my body throbbing – I almost let go.

I've really gotta go.

Okay.

Okay.

I moved off the stoop and felt about eighty years old. I creaked. It hurt.

Okay. Well. Bye, I said, ready to stay.

Bye, he said, and he gave me one last tiny slow soft kiss which was all I needed, before he headed off on his way.

David Hass

David Hass is a psychotherapist who began life as an actor and writer and is now returning to his roots.

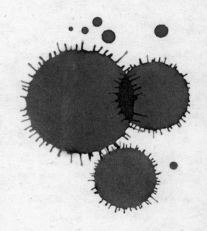

Remember Me

A Story

> . . . remember thee?
> Ay, thou poor ghost . . .
> I have sworn it.
> *Hamlet, Act I Scene V*

I spoke to a friend about my attempts to do some 'life writing'. He said, 'Why do you call it that? Life writing is just a neologism for what used to be called "confessional writing"' – and he cited Rousseau.

Later, I thought, yes, along with the impulse to attest to having been here, and most of all, the time-honoured impulse to tell a story, it is also a confession. But to whom is one confessing? Surely not to the as yet indifferent, imaginary readership. Even then, embedded in the story, it could only be incidentally that. However, as I began to write, I gradually learned that once you start to probe and excavate you come to understand that it is to yourself you are confessing.

At first I wanted to write a love story – perhaps about marriage, perhaps about my ex-wife – and then about the death of marriage even while love still exists. But slowly another story took shape and I wasn't certain whether it would turn into a love story – or be just a story about love. It was an account of childhood – and I was reminded of the steel thread that binds the various bits of our pasts together, and how often we are forced to reconnect to childhood even as we try to escape it. In the end, I found there were two stories, tangentially linked.

I begin with a brief section of the first story – the one which comes from my marriage.

David Hass

Anna

We met when we were both appearing in fringe plays at the
Edinburgh Festival. I had come over with an off-Broadway troupe.
She was appearing in a play with a local company. Her name was
Anna. She was Scottish-Italian-Catholic – both parents had emi-
grated from Italy. I was American-Jewish, but her family, particularly the extended family of aunts, uncles, cousins, were in
temperament and character totally familiar to me.

I was twenty-two, Anna was twenty, and as the pop songs say,
I looked into her eyes and found love at first sight. Oddly enough,
although I couldn't exactly place them, I knew those eyes. They are
the kind of eyes I always succumb to: large, generous, dark, dark
brown – and you can always tell what they are thinking – but sometimes when the light moves on and a shadow covers them, they turn
ink black. It is then that their look is indecipherable – then, that
they hold on to their secrets and give nothing away.

But it is the second story – the one on childhood – that I want to
tell first.

Childhood

Everyone in the gang on the street called each other by diminu-
tives, all ending with the sound of 'e'. We were Marty, Freddie,
Danny, Jerry and later when he came to live on the street, there
was Louie.

Eventually, Louie and I became best friends, and sometimes I was
razzed by the others, when as an in-joke referring to Louie's Italian
origin, they named me 'Martini'. I didn't mind because my family
also called me Marty, and Martini was a name that belonged to the
street – the property of the gang. When coupled with Louie, it had
a nice vaudevillian ring. 'Louie and Martini', 'Martini and Louie' –
like a soft-shoe double act. Before Louie came to the street, there
were just the four of us – too few in number to constitute a real
gang – nor were we really old enough to want to identify ourselves

as such. We were plain friends – playmates from the same street and classmates from the same class at P.S. 33. That was the bond.

Our street was Walton Avenue – the north end at East 184th. My house – a six-storey walk-up – was just around the corner. We lived on the top floor – a three-room apartment with windows to the front – my parents, my older sister Rachel, and me. My mother said she would never live in the back and though it was hard walking up six flights of stairs, she needed the front to look out and see the world. The truth was that the higher up you were, the cheaper the rent. Still, we were lucky. It was the Depression and my father had a good job behind the counter at Harvey's Kosher Delicatessen and Diner, so we could pay the rent and we ate well.

Jerry Pearlman's house was the second down on the block – like ours, a six-storey walk-up – only they lived on the third floor. Jerry's father wore a skull cap and owned the kosher butcher premises in the big covered market at 183rd Street. Sometimes, during the High Holy Days, Mrs Pearlman helped out. My mother bought her weekly ration of freshly ground meat from Pearlman's, which she fed to us uncooked, for reasons of health, mixed with raw onions and raw potatoes – her grandmother's recipe from the old country and a treasured tradition. We loved it and seemed to thrive.

Further down, in one of the remaining tenements, was Freddie Schwartz. His father was a bus driver and his mother worked selling groceries at the local A&P on Jerome Avenue – opposite the El. Mr Schwartz was also a Union leader and involved in strikes. They had a cold water flat heated by paraffin stoves, and they washed in the kitchen sink and shared a toilet with another family on the landing.

Just opposite, across the street, was Danny Siegel's house. This was an eight-storey building and the only one on the block that had an elevator. The Siegels occupied a duplex, in which his father, who was a dentist, had his office. The duplex had a sunken living room with sky-blue wall-to-wall carpet. You had to walk down three steps and there was a small curved iron railing on each side.

Danny's mother made you take your shoes off before you were allowed down, so you had to make sure your socks had no holes when you visited. That was how we found out that Anton Buchmann, from Burnside Avenue, the Norwegian kid in our class who sometimes joined us, wore only the tops of socks and had bare feet inside his ankle boots – even in winter. Anton's father was out of work and his mother was sick – 'mentally', my mother had heard. The Welfare Department looked after them and they lived on Relief.

What distinguished Walton from the others in the neighbourhood was that it was still a street in transition. The surrounding areas, like Morris Avenue – which ran parallel to Walton – were already built up. On Morris all the apartment houses were new – all with elevators, some with doormen. Walton still had surviving tenements, like the one Freddie lived in, but they were scheduled to be knocked down. Six tenements had already been knocked down near the 183rd Street end and left a huge empty lot, where in the summer we played baseball.

It was hard to imagine, when we studied local history in school, how our street would have looked to Johannes Bronkas after he had founded the Bronx. The only evidence that rural life ever existed was a giant oak tree which stood near the kerb of the sidewalk opposite the Pearlmans' house. The branches were so high up, Mrs Pearlman complained that in the summer, when the leaves were out, it made her kitchen dark.

We never climbed the tree – warned off by the tale of a boy who had once fallen off and broken both legs, never to walk again. Only the dogs used it to pee against – and once a cat got stuck and had to be rescued by the Fire Department. This caused much excitement and was even mentioned in the weekly *Bronx Home News*.

In the summer – and childhood in those days seemed mostly summer – the sidewalk was our playground. The boys played box-ball and shot marbles, the girls 'potsy' and jump-rope. And when we were even younger and not self-conscious about boys and girls playing together, it was 'giants' and 'follow the leader' and 'hide and seek'.

However, our greatest delight was on the dog days when the New York humidity had extinguished even our indomitable energies and the police opened the fire hydrants. We were instantly rejuvenated – jumping out of our clothes, pushing and shoving, dodging gleefully in and out of the path of the gushing water.

They were good summers – the best – but they changed as our bodies changed. Summers could continue to be good, but they would never again be so untroubled.

Louie

One August, just after I had my tenth birthday, the Francesco family moved into the janitor's basement quarters in the house next door to Jerry. Mr Francesco, the new janitor, had two daughters: Elena who was fourteen, Renata who was four, and he had a son, Louie, who was ten, like me. There was no mother.

The Francescos were Italian and Catholic. We were all Russian or Polish Jews. It was Louie's 'foreignness' that immediately drew us to him. There is a picture of him that often comes into my mind: it is a winter picture. New York winters are bitterly cold and along with our scarves, lumber jackets, leggings and galoshes when it snowed, we all had hand-knitted or store-bought woolly hats pulled tightly over our ears. Louie wore none of these. Instead, he had a brown leather bombardier's jacket with a goat-skin lining – and on his head, seeming to complement his dark brown eyes, was a black felt beret. We kids were all proud first-generation Americans and no American boy that we knew would ever wear a beret. It had been his father's, and brought from the old country. It looked new and somehow managed to go on fitting year after year. It seemed to sum up Louie's 'foreignness' for us, part of what made him exotic and different – the insignia of his romance.

Louie possessed another mystery which both intrigued and frightened us: his mother was dead and we couldn't imagine how anyone could live without a mother. Usually, it was too scary to think about, but sometimes when he wasn't there, we speculated about what it might be like. Louie never mentioned his mother.

But we got to know some of the story because Louie's sister Elena and my sister Rachel were in the same class in high school and had become friends.

Elena told my sister that their mother had died in childbirth when Renata was born. Louie was six at the time and she, ten. Since Renata had never known her mother, she didn't miss her as they did – though she asked about her sometimes. For a while, their aunt had come to look after them, then she left to get married – but that was all right since she and Louie were that much older by then, and they helped their father care for Renata.

Before moving to Walton, the Francescos lived on the Lower East Side near family and friends, where Mr Francesco was the janitor of a small apartment house. He had been a janitor ever since coming to America, but he mainly earned his living by furniture repairs, mending broken chairs and table legs, and also by cane weaving. But one day, Elena said, he decided that he had too many sad memories, living there where their mother had died, and he needed to move away and leave the memories behind. So they came to Walton, though it was a bigger house to look after, which left him less time to do his repairs. Still she and Louie helped a lot – and Mr Francesco had begun to sing again. It was true. Mr Francesco had a powerful tenor. He was like a story-book Italian and sang *O sole mio* and *La donna è mobile* in a loud resounding voice, which on certain days could be heard around the block. It was generally when he was putting out the trash cans full of ashes from the boiler for the twice-weekly garbage collections. Sometimes Louie accompanied him and sometimes you could hear him singing too, though not so loud. They were both sunny, father and son, that's how you could describe them. In winter, hearing them sing, my mother would say, 'They bring the sun from Italy to warm us up.'

Louie did well in school, even with so much to do at home. The rest of us had household tasks like going to the bakery on 183rd and buying bread or taking the laundry to the laundromat down the road. But Louie had adult chores. Before and after school, he helped look after the house. In the morning, he mopped the stoop and when he came home, he swept the vestibule. He did this quickly so he could come out to play. But he was back every night at six o'clock sharp to pull the dumbwaiter and collect the tenants' garbage so his father could feed the boiler. He also ran errands to the shops for the tenants and made tips. This was how he was able to save and buy little presents for his sister, Renata, whom he loved so.

Renata was like Louie: always smiling, always sunny. She had a disarming way of rushing into your arms whenever she saw you – planting a kiss on your cheek, demanding a cuddle, a swing-round, a piggy-back. She treated the street as a trusted extended family – and the street, in turn, gave her its heart.

Elena was friendly, but grave, as though her responsibilities would not permit light-heartedness. She attended to the family's practical needs: the sewing, the ironing – and provided the comfort for the small everyday things that befell: the knocks, the falls. It was Elena's job to take Renata to kindergarten each morning. Mr Francesco would pick her up after school because Elena, like my sister, might be staying on. There were various activities to join, such as the Drama Society and the Glee Club, to which they both belonged. Her father shopped, but Elena did most of the cooking.

Mr Francesco worked hardest of all. There were six flights of stairs and six floors to sweep and mop each day and the windows on the landings to wash weekly. There were also the repairs, fixing the fuses, replacing the lights and most important, making sure the boiler never stopped working for the hot water and in winter for the central heating.

Mr Rosenthal, who was Mr Francesco's boss and our landlord too, told my mother, when he came to collect the rent, that he wished all the janitors of the buildings he owned worked as hard as Mr Francesco. The hall floors were mopped so clean you could eat off them.

He took one day off, Sunday, to go to church with the children and spend the afternoon visiting his sisters or brothers in Manhattan or New Jersey.

Sometimes, Louie would stay behind and join me and the others going to the movies. My sister Rachel had just got her part-time state work-permit and had a weekend job as an usherette at the Lido Theater. She would get us in free to the first afternoon showing on Sunday and that was how we got to see Errol Flynn as Robin Hood – and that's how, when we finally became a genuine gang, we called ourselves the Walton Merry Men.

The Merry Men

The summer after Louie arrived, we were about the age gangs generally get going. As Louie had a pre-eminence among us, he became our leader. It was his idea that we be the Merry Men and his idea to challenge the gang from Morris Avenue for the exclusive use of the empty lot for our ball games throughout the vacation. We knew the kids on Morris. They were also Russian/Polish Jews and some were in our class. We decided not to have a punch-up, but to use weapons. We filched stockings from our mothers or sisters, filling the sock part with flour and rushed at one another like knights wielding their maces in a medieval tournament. The loser had to cry 'Uncle'. However, in addition to surrendering the lot, there was a further penalty thought up by the Morris gang – the losing team had to have their pants pulled down and their cocks checked out.

We flew into battle with great energy. The only rule we made was that nobody was allowed to punch or scratch, though we could trip each other up. The battle raged for a quarter of an hour, with lots of whooping and shouting – white powder blurring our vision – more like Red Indians than knights. Though we fought fiercely, Morris Avenue were more expert as trippers-up – and we were forced ignobly to the ground, crying 'Uncle' and conceding defeat.

Losing the lot was shame-making enough and yet to come were the excuses we would have to make to our families explaining away the state of our powder-white clothing – but, of course, worst of all was the impending humiliation of pulling down our pants. Though we were all completely innocent and more or less ignorant of sexual matters, there was nevertheless a nervous unease about our genitals. Were they too small – were they even too large? And what if someone should see what we were doing – what would our parents say? However there was no way out of it. Morris Avenue demanded we honour our agreement.

Although we were far back from the sidewalk, we formed a close circle so that no grown-up passing by could see us. One by one we dropped our pants and were checked out. We were very quick – what if someone caught us? – but when it was Louie's turn to be checked out, there was a long pause. He was uncircumcised. 'That's a funny one,' someone said. A red blush spread over Louie's face. My heart went out to him in his humiliation. I said, 'What's so funny about it, maybe yours is the funny one.' A silence ensued – everyone seemed to be considering this. Finally, Jerry said, 'Let's go. I gotta be home.' We disbanded – the winning warriors marching up to Morris, the Merry Men sheepishly dragging their feet, worrying how their dishevelled appearances would be received. Louie and I walked together. He put his arm over my shoulder – and it was the same every time we met thereafter. We walked with his arm over my shoulder.

Release

In our last year in elementary school before transferring to Junior High, a new addition to the school curriculum was introduced, called Religious Release. On Tuesday afternoons, between two and three o'clock, you could leave the school premises and go to your chosen institution for 'religious instruction', or you could stay in school and continue with ordinary work. With the prospect of leaving school early, practically everyone elected for religious release – except Freddie, on principle. His parents didn't believe in God, he said. He stayed in school.

I enrolled at the Hebrew School in the small shop-fronted 'Shul' on 179th Street. Louie went to his church on Valentine Avenue a few streets away. Danny attended the fee-paying Synagogue School on the Grand Concourse, and Jerry used the time to work at the market and make deliveries for his father.

Louie and I would both get out around four o'clock. I always waited for him outside the Shul so we could walk home together. One day, his usually smiling face looked serious as he came to meet me. He didn't put his arm around my shoulder. Something was up. 'What's wrong?' I asked. 'Nothing,' he said, and we walked silently for a while. Then he said, 'The Jews killed Christ.' A kind of terror shot through me. 'No, they didn't,' I said. 'Yes they did,' he insisted and stopped walking as if to make the point. The terror gripped me and I wanted to say something to Louie which would bring his arm back round my shoulder, but instead I heard myself say, 'So what if they did?'

Louie sprang at me and I toppled to the ground, my head luckily landing on my arm. Then I felt his knee in my chest – pressing hard. 'Say you're sorry,' he said. He brought his face close to mine. The colour of his eyes seemed to have darkened with hate. I couldn't believe he had this feeling – surely it couldn't be just because I was Jewish? Why, I wanted to ask – but now his face came so close to mine, I could feel his breath. 'Say sorry,' he repeated and twisted my arm with such force that the pain drew the words from me.

He stood up. I lay shaking – but felt wild with rage and getting to my knees, grabbed at his leg, knocking him off guard. His body hit the ground with a thud. Our positions were now reversed, and I was on top of him. 'You bastard,' I shouted, 'you bastard,' and I found I was choking him. I saw tears forming in his eyes. 'Don't,' he whispered. 'Don't.' He could only just get the words out. I let go. He lay absolutely still – winded. I stretched out next to him and began to sob.

It was like a seepage from a torn heart which would never get right again. Eventually he touched my arm and I heard him say, 'It's okay. It's okay.'

When I stopped, I couldn't look at him. I got up and walked away. He caught up with me. 'Wait,' he said, touching my arm. We walked silently. What's happened, I wondered? What's going to happen now? As we approached our street, he began to whistle – a soft whistle so you could hardly hear it. Then he put his arm over my shoulder. I bit my lips – there were more tears coming. 'You know,' he said, suddenly cheerful, 'that wasn't so bad. We didn't really hurt each other. We could do more wrestling, you know. We don't have to hurt each other. It could be good fun.'

The Gladiators

We never spoke about what happened that afternoon. I could sense that Louie never wanted to. It was like the subject of his mother – a taboo. And my own feelings were confused. Deep down, there was resentment. It had been unjust. How could I help being Jewish? But I knew there was something more than that – what was that sudden look of hate as he lay on top of me? There had been another message in his eyes. In some way, I was relieved that we would never talk about it.

And we did wrestle again – every week – on Tuesday after Hebrew and Catholic School and on Sunday mornings when Louie got back from church. It became a ritual. We went to Van Cortlandt Park and found an isolated patch, flat and grassy, and wrestled there. We got good at not hurting each other. Sometimes Freddie, Jerry and Danny came with us. Freddie and Jerry joined in, but Danny would come only to watch. He didn't join in as he was going to be a dentist when he grew up like his father and he was afraid of injuring his hands.

When we were twelve, we transferred to Crescent Junior High School. Louie and I joined the Wrestling Team. The coach, Mr Simons, called us 'The Gladiators'. He treated wrestling like a science – like in our chemistry class – teaching us what was safe and was not safe to try.

We discovered that everything we had done instinctively – all the moves we had worked out for ourselves – had names. This delighted us. There was the 'Bridge Back': your arms around the opponent's chest, legs around the thighs. Then there was the 'Sprawl': arms around the back, legs around the ankles. There were a lot: the Knee Lock, the Underarm Spin, the True Cross Body Pin, the Cradle and many more. There were dozens to remember as Mr Simons barked them out. We knew them all. Our movements went from crude to almost refined. We could be rough and we could also be graceful. And when it happened, there was the thrill of the victor over the vanquished. 'Submit' was the official word of submission from your opponent. But for some reason, Louie and I continued to use 'say Uncle' between ourselves. And all the time, our bodies were growing and filling out. When we were fourteen, in our last year, we had reached puberty and the height and frame we were to be as adults. You could say we grew up wrestling.

We forgot about the empty lot. During the summer vacation – the summer before transferring to High School – after Louie's morning chores, he and I went to Van Cortlandt Park. We went most days to the park. Freddie and Jerry had taken summer jobs delivering in the market. Every day Louie and I wrestled – then we swam – then we lay about, speculating about the future. I already knew I wanted to be an actor. Louie didn't know – but he wasn't very ambitious: a fireman, maybe a cop, even a soldier. He loved uniforms. But mainly we talked about High School, wondering about the older kids and whether there would be bullies. We worried if we would be tough enough. We worried – but we basked in the sun, which burned and then tanned our skins. After each match, we were less fatigued, we could go on for longer. We exulted in our stamina.

One day, we were walking home from the park, as usual. Louie had his arm round my shoulder. On Fordham and the Grand Concourse, an ambulance passed us with its siren blasting. We took no particular notice. We were near home, just crossing Morris, when Jerry seemed to come at us from nowhere. He had been waiting, he said. There was bad news. Renata had been taken away in an ambulance to Fordham Hospital. She had been run over.

We ran down the hill and round the corner. A small group of neighbours including my mother and Mrs Pearlman had gathered in front of the house. It was true. 'Your father and Elena are at the hospital,' Mrs Pearlman said to Louie.

It was a common enough story. You read about it in the papers every day. She had been playing with a ball. It rolled into the road. She ran to retrieve it. The car couldn't brake in time.

My mother pressed a five-dollar bill into my hand. 'Here,' she said. 'Take a taxi. Go with him.'

I knew Fordham Hospital. It's where I had my tonsils out when I was five, and my mother's cousin, Hymie, died there in the Crippling Diseases ward. We were directed to the Emergency Wing – hope and doom alternating inside us, first one and then the other – but I somehow knew it was doom even before I saw Mr Francesco, his arms folding around a weeping Elena. They did not see us. Louie did not move. Then he turned and threw himself into my arms, quietly sobbing. It was the first time anyone had ever sought me out for comfort – used my body as a refuge. I was almost as grieved as Louie. I loved Renata too – but all the feeling I had, all the strength I owned, went into holding him – knowing it was useless – but trying to ward off – shield him from his pain.

Goodbyes

The funeral was the following week. But in an unexpected way our religions became a divide. The Jewish families felt ignorant of the right protocol. They knew there was a vigil. Many family and friends of the Francescos never seen before came to the house. Someone saw a priest go in. The Jewish neighbours wrote letters of condolence and put them under the door – but as Jews they thought it would be disrespectful to intrude further. It was a private grief – and a grief which had an alien ritual to attend it.

The street mourned for Renata. My mother said she would be an angel. Children who died before the age of nine, before the age of moral responsibility, became angels. It was found in all religions, she said.

I waited for a sign from Louie. I hadn't seen him since the hospital. I agonised over what to do. Did he want me with him? They would be polite, but would the family think me out of place? In the end, I succumbed to a kind of inertia – unable to do anything but wait. But no sign came. After the funeral I avoided going around the corner when I went out.

About three weeks later, my mother came home with the news that the Francescos were moving. She had met Mr Francesco in the market. He poured out his grief to her. He was finished, he said. He couldn't do it alone any more. He was moving to be near his sister and her family in Dover, New Jersey. He had found a job there in a new apartment building. At first he thought he would stay to let Elena finish High School – but he couldn't. That was the way he had to deal with it. When his parents died, he came to America; when his wife died, he moved from Manhattan to the Bronx; and now he had to move again to where there could be no reminders. He would sell all the furniture. He would begin again. A broken heart did not kill you. It only crippled you. You limped through life. There was no more dancing and now there would be no more singing either – no, his Renata had taken his voice with her.

I was alone the next day when the door bell rang. My mother had just gone out. I knew it would be Louie. I knew he'd waited until he saw my mother leave the house. 'We're moving tomorrow,' he said. 'I've come to say goodbye.' He told me about Dover, New Jersey, what a good place it would be, near his aunts and cousins. He'd seen the new High School – anyway, New Jersey was not that far away – he'd be back and I could come to visit.

All the while he spoke, his eyes were turned away. He was looking out the window. I was afraid to feel. I was afraid to speak. Finally, I put my hand on his shoulder and said, 'I'll miss you.' He turned round – his dark, dark eyes glistened behind tears. He looked at me for a long time. It was not exactly a stare – but as if he were trying to make up his mind to say something more – but he needed some kind of clue before going on. 'What?' I asked – trying to decipher the question in his eyes. But then as though he had willed a trick of light, a shadow fell across his eyes and I could read nothing. 'I better be going,' he said and opened the door. 'I'll never wrestle again,' I said. He turned and smiled at me and then went out.

Growing Up

I never did wrestle again. For a while, I couldn't bear to have anyone even touch me. In High School, I joined the Drama Club and the Fencing Society. Fencing, like wrestling, was a dance for two, but the object was always to be beyond touch.

Louie and I never met again – though nothing stopped us. Elena sent a Christmas card with their address. She and my sister met up a couple of times. I heard Louie was doing well.

I missed him after he left. When I turned the corner, I half expected to run into him. There were lots of people there – but it was an empty street. The others were more or less gone too. We all went to different schools. Sometimes we'd see each other, wave or stop. 'How's it going?' It was always, 'Okay.' – 'See you.' Was it Louie who had kept us together for so long?

But the pace of adolescence and its demands was a great healer. There were new friends, then sex and girlfriends – I had my adolescent crushes – and there were studies – and then acting, which totally absorbed me.

I thought of Louie from time to time, wondering how he was – but then less and less. Twice, I saw him from a distance. Once he was sitting below me in the bleachers at the Yankee Stadium, but by the time I pushed my way through the crowds after the game, he was gone. A couple of years after that – I must have been around nineteen – I glimpsed him on the IRT platform at 14th Street as the train was pulling out. He was standing with a girl with long black hair. He had his arm around her waist and they were both laughing. I was attending weekly drama classes at the New School, so 14th Street was my station, and for a couple of weeks I looked for him when I got off and on. Then one day, absorbed in remembering some lines, I forgot to look – and then, some months later, it crossed my mind that I had forgotten completely.

Remember Me

After a number of years of living in England, Martin and his wife came to visit New York. They came primarily to see his mother and father who had now moved to an Assisted Housing Estate in Lower Manhattan and to see his sister, who was married and lived on Riverside Drive. Rachel seemed happy with her life. Both she and her husband, Charlie, who was from upstate New York, taught history – she at Hunter, he at C.C.N.Y. Martin planned to stay two weeks. Rachel was putting them up.

The first night, reminiscing about the Bronx over a glass of wine, Rachel said, 'Oh, by the way, do you remember that kid, Louie Francesco? I was friends with his sister Elena at high school. Wasn't he a friend of yours?' She had heard, she said, from someone, she couldn't remember how, that he was dead – killed in Vietnam. 'Can you believe such a thing? He was married and had a kid. A little girl – but he volunteered.'

'He always thought he might become a soldier,' Martin said, but his first thought had been of Louie's father – maybe if he had been granted any luck in life, Mr Francesco would have long been dead before Louie had died.

Martin lay awake. They were in the spare room. The hum of traffic on the Drive just reached him. His sister's apartment was on the twelfth floor. If he got up and went to the window and pulled up the shade, he would be able to see the river and perhaps make out the Palisades on the Jersey side. Riverside Drive was just a subway ride from where they grew up – but it was a ride he would never take again.

'Jersey' – that's where the Francesco family had moved to when Renata died. What happened afterwards? Was his wife that pretty girl he'd seen him with on the IRT platform – laughing together. He wondered – if he were to see her, would he be able to catch a glimpse of Louie's face in the face of his daughter?

His wife's voice startled him. He had been so much in his own thoughts, that he had almost forgotten that she was there sleeping beside him. 'A penny for your thoughts,' she asked. 'I'm not think-ing anything,' he said quickly – and wondered if he had spoken too sharply. He felt a momentary confusion as though caught in an act of concealment. More softly he said, 'Go back to sleep, darling, I'm okay – just getting used to being back.' He heard her sigh and turn over. She could always sense his unease. Presently, he could tell by her breathing that she was asleep.

'A penny for your thoughts.' What were your thoughts, Louie, those last minutes? Was there even time to think? Did your life flash up and rush before you like they say it does? Did a memory of me flicker there?

He thought he was going to sob, but held back. He mustn't wake her. This was not something he could ever share. He searched the dark. The lights from the street shone faintly from behind the window shade. He rested his eyes there. What am I looking for? he asked himself – but he knew what he was looking for.

Now Martin shut his eyes. He needn't strain them any more searching in the dark. He could see what he needed to see with them closed. He saw the two boys – Louie and himself. He saw them outside the Hebrew School – he saw them as adolescents on the isolated green patch in Van Cortlandt Park. They were laughing – they were wrestling – taking turns in winning and losing – taking turns in pinning each other down. 'Say Uncle' – and they pressed their bodies harder into each other. 'Say Uncle,' as they crushed the breath out from one another. 'Uncle,' one would finally whisper – and for a moment longer they lay clasped together – a single corpse – before there was energy enough to disentangle and move away.

This time he did sob aloud, but only once. Louie, he whispered, into the dark. He got up quietly, moved from the bed and lay down on the floor. He was shivering. Louie, he whispered again.

It was like a dream. He felt a presence lying beside him – without looking, he knew it was Louie's body. Was this why, he thought? Is it this body that had always forced a space between the many bodies he had pinned down in the years that followed, when he had yearned so much to close the space between their bodies and his own? Was this why?

Now Martin understood the question hidden in Louie's eyes. He turned to the body beside him. 'Louie,' he whispered. 'Forgive me.'

Now Martin looked into the soft dark eyes of his Doppelganger – and the ghost entered, embraced and reclaimed its flesh.

Myrlin Hermes

Myrlin Hermes was born in California in 1975. She is the author of the novel *Careful What You Wish For* and recipient of the 2004 IHS Film and Fiction Award. 'Wodan's Wound' is an excerpt from her second novel.

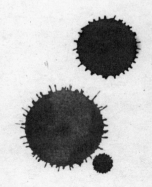

Wodan's Wound

The castle Elsinore, seen from the sea, at first looks like nothing so much as a smudge on the face of the water, a trick of the light. The light plays the sort of tricks here that send shudders down sailors' spines – particularly in these last and coldest hours of the night. In summer, in these northern lands, the grey shadow of dawn begins to creep into the sky long before the sun stirs. You might think you saw anything at all in that fine pale mist, in the broken surf the colour of iron and ice.

But it is not only the eye that is tricked here; and it is not the thought of pirates or sea-serpents or the toll in gold taxed by the king for passing through the Sound that makes sailors whisper a prayer to themselves as they find their ships approaching Elsinore. It is the low moaning that rises off the cliffs, like the ghostly noise of sailors, lost in the flotsam of ancient wrecks. Or you might think it was a baby's cry, carried in fragments over the sea by a chance wind, or the voice of a despairing young girl, singing to herself broken bits of old love songs. These are not the sirens, luring men to their deaths with whispered promises of love and rest. No – these ghosts wail all human anguish, cry out for assistance, for revenge. These voices draw you in with their despair, their bottomless need. Everyone hears something different in the cliffs of Elsinore, and even those sceptics who claim it is merely the breeze playing pan-pipes at the mouths of sea-caves will admit it is an eerie music. No one who has heard the sound ever forgets it, and everyone arriving at the castle spends the first few nights sleepless but for bad dreams.

It is the sea here, the terrible sea. The gods of a land are born out of its horizon – its marriage of earth and sky, of water and sunrise. And this is no sparkling Mediterranean, to give rise to Apollos, to beautiful deities made of music and light. No, the gods of these waters are gods of thunder, gods of revenge. Elemental tricksters, weary warriors, they bear scars of ancient wounds. They are missing hands and eyes. They understand that Heaven is another battlefield, and know that no wisdom worth having ever comes without a price.

The King of Denmark understands this more deeply than he knows it. In his blood and bone, his body bears witness to the history of his land. Like his ancestors, those proud Vikings, he is great in both stature and girth, with a sable beard that once would have been the making of his name. A grey mist hangs low over the water, grazing the masts of the ships gathered and ready to sail at dawn for the disputed colonies to the north.

Two sailors lead between them to the beach a sleepy-looking ewe, the sacrifice to consecrate their endeavour. Though each of the men has made his confessions to his church, entrusting his soul to Heaven should he die in the conflict, summoning the winds for the journey requires an older magic – transmutations more complex than wine from water, or blood from wine. The king's ancestors nod in recognition as he prepares the ritual, which, though the name of St Michael has replaced that of the pagan god, has remained otherwise unaltered for thousands of years.

And, though the king is a Christian, the paradise he anticipates resembles in all but name the great palace, Valhalla. His forefathers did not fear death, except a coward's death – succumbing to the ravages of illness or old age. A warrior who returned triumphant from every battlefield was cursed as much as blessed, to witness in comfort his own decline. For such a hero who found himself on his deathbed and wished to join at the immortals' table, it was no shame to seek his own remedy with a small incision by spearpoint, called Wodan's wound.

But that was long ago; these days, the church's views on suicide are clear. And though the king has been assured many times by his confessor that it is no less heroic to die in one's bed than one's boots, and his soul will in either case find its final reward, still this morning he is awake before the sun, in full armour, pacing the cliffs by the beach. In the tender light, he might yet pass for a man half his age, the silver in his famous black beard mistaken for sea-salt or hoar-frost.

The Council, sensing that His Majesty was bent on war whether they approved or disapproved, had made valiant attempts to dissuade him from leading the fleet himself. At his age, they protested, surely he had earned a respite from the battlefield – for, though this campaign has been referred to always as an investigative visit from the monarch, anyone with an eye left in his head can see these ships are armed for an attack.

But he insisted. It was thirty years ago when, leading a similar convoy, he first took the territories from Fortinbras, himself delivering on that lord the fatal blow. Now the king has had word of the son gathering an army, rising to take back the land his father lost. Another Fortinbras, like those ancient monsters who grew another head as soon as the hero had cut off the first. To whom besides himself (the king demanded of his men) could it be more sweet and fitting for the task to fall of sending Fortinbras, son of Fortinbras, to his father's fate?

His advisers wisely resisted the obvious answer. The king's only legitimate son is rather a sore subject with the monarch. Though intended, like his father, to follow a military career as soon as his education is completed, the prince has lingered so long in school he might be accused of malingering – or else, it is joked, he must surely have earned his professorship by now. And the reports and rumours arriving from Wittenberg of the prodigal son's antics there – while impressing the impressionable young ladies of the court – serve in the soldiers' barracks only to make the prince even more of a laughingstock. Not that young Hamlet is ever called a coward outright. Treason, of course, to think of it that way.

They are gathering now on the shore, the king's soldiers, standing in twos and threes together smoking, not speaking, stamping their feet in the cold. They practise the feints and parries they have learned, or check their armour; archers test their strings in the damp air. Some have served beside the king for many years, in many wars; others are scarcely half the age of his delinquent son. Those too young to grow a beard wear their helmets with the beaver plates (so called for the fur lining) down to disguise this fact. The king nods his head to these boys as he passes. They would return from this combat men, or not at all. This strikes him as meet, a fitting trial to test who among them deserved the privileges of manhood.

He gives the signal. The horn is sounded. The sun is beginning to rise. The ewe bleats as a dim suspicion of her destiny begins to cross the vast untended pasture of her mind. Finally, she struggles and tries to run – far too late. The purpose of the knife is unmistakable. The soldiers gather around as the king prepares the rites of war.

At first, the only sign of a wind is a gentle breeze from the south, which barely swells their sails into bellies, but carries a heady scent. The cherry trees in the king's private walled orchard have come into bloom, glistening with dew like a fresh late snowfall.

But the woman slipping across the parapeted terrace down to the gardens and into this picturesque scene – a fur cloak wrapped around her head and shoulders, her fair hair undone – is unaware of the abundance of scent around her, and for the most prosaic of reasons: she has been crying, and her nose is stuffed up.

From another world, a hundred yards away, she hears the call of the horn; the sheep's fatal scream. She draws more tightly around herself the robe – which on second glance reveals itself to be a coronation mantle, lined in ermine.

On St Valentine's day, they say, the first lady a bachelor spies in the morning is destined to be his true-love. Many a maid may be seen wandering about before dawn under particular windows, hoping to influence the fates in their choice. But the calendar is already several months past that saint's day; and this figure, though slender in her night-rail, is similarly advanced past maidenhood, into (she is already weeping; we shall be delicate) the very late summer of life. Her son, after all, is thirty this year; and the Queen of Denmark, though married young, had been no child-bride.

The queen – this is even how she thinks of herself. Often she will forget for days at a time that she ever had another name. Gertrude was someone else: a young and pretty girl – a distant relative, perhaps? a niece? – whom the queen remembers fondly, but not often. For three decades she has been called 'Your Majesty', or 'Madam'. Even her husband, who might have addressed her more intimately, has never in all her memory used her Christian name. Instead he calls her by the generic 'Wife'; or else he refers obliquely to her relationship as queen of his country, mother to his son – parties by whom his own perception of her is always triangulated.

Early this morning, stirred by a late night of drinking, with each toast to the success of his campaign punctuated by cannonfire, he visited her bedchamber to perform upon her his conjugal duties. A private passageway has been constructed for this purpose between the king's bed-closet and the queen's, concealed at either end by heavy French tapestries. He likes to slip in after she has already fallen asleep, to take her by surprise. She woke with the crush of his body upon her, blotting out the sky. He likes to feel her struggle, though her strength is nothing to his and he easily subdues her. The queen is a practical woman, and has learned the tricks of a whore. If she does what pleases him, she knows it will be over more quickly. She wraps her legs around him in response to his breathless prompts, hissing hysterical confessions of lust.

Later, she will hardly remember the things she said; though fragments of the phrases would repeat themselves without warning in her head days or weeks later, like memories of shameful dreams. Nor would she mention it to her confessor. God knows what He knows, she trusts, and will judge accordingly. Besides, as any footman in the castle can tell you, the chapel echoes badly, and is rife with eavesdroppers.

When the king was done, he pulled away and threw the bed-curtains back, examining her naked body in the candlelight. The bruises he left had been deliberately placed; nothing about his handiwork is sloppy, in love or war. He noted the positioning of each of them, the little red berry-marks raised by his signet ring on her white breasts. While he sails to Norway, he will remember each and every mark, imagining the bruises fading, their edges yellowing, taking a greenish tint beneath the skin; and in this way will he be able to imagine his influence upon her even when he is gone. He ran his hand over her bare white body as if looking at a map of a battlefield laid out, on a territory belonging to himself alone. Then he kissed her once on the lips and dressed, his mind already gone ahead to his preparations of war.

The queen lay in the bed until he was gone. Then she began to weep silently, the way she has learned to do so as not to wake the guard outside her door. She has wept every night before her husband sailed away to war; and even after three decades she could not tell you whether it is fear or sorrow or relief that brings this flood of tears into her eyes. She speaks to herself quite sternly: *No use crying now. What's done is done. Best make the best of it.*

No use trying to sleep, either. When she was certain he would be gone with the soldiers, she slipped through the very passageway through which he had come to her, through his rooms, which showed evidence of finality and haste. Not until she saw his coronation mantle, draped with some ceremony across the bed, did she realise she was shivering. Gathering the mantle around her shoulders, she made her way through the neighbouring room and down the steps leading out into the king's private orchard.

Anyone seeing her there in her nightgown, fair hair undone in a tangle of frizzy pale curls, might suspect the queen of somnambulism, or madness. A slightly lazy eye gives her a dull, befuddled look, as though she were always dreaming. In her youth this only magnified her ethereal beauty, but it has worsened as she has aged, especially when she is tired or under stress.

She was once the Belle of Elsinore, and at her best (which at the moment she cannot be said to be) the queen is still a lovely woman; but hers is that fair and rosy sort of beauty which is at its peak in the ingénue; and which loses something priceless and intangible when it ceases to be effortless. Her full cheeks have begun to hint at jowlsiness at the jaw – as her husband loves to remind her, pinching at a fingerful of the offending flesh. In subtler ways he reminds her as well, silently, with his roving eye: never again will she be the most interesting woman in any room.

And as for himself? The queen looks at her husband sometimes and wonders how he can have remained so completely unchanged, after all these years. Broader in the belly, yes, and greyer in the beard, but still the same man she married, *cap-à-pie*. She can see in him sometimes the young war hero with whom she fell in love; who returned triumphant from battle after battle, beaming, his good-will casting a genial glow over everything. And he is still that person, when everything goes his way. When his armies are winning, his sleep undisturbed, his soup hot, his ale cold, and his will unquestioningly and swiftly obeyed, the king is as sunny and charming a man as one could hope to meet. It is merely when any-thing at all goes wrong that he becomes awful to everyone. A lost battle, a lost key, a saucy letter from the prince, even a bout of indi-gestion is enough to cast a cloud over him: a silent rage hangs about his head, ready to strike out at whatever or whoever is careless enough to catch his attention.

For the most part, everyone at court tries to ensure that nothing ever goes wrong. Misplaced possessions are swiftly found and replaced, errors are corrected or covered up. A whispered word of warning is passed on days when his mood is black, and instantly everyone makes themselves scarce. The queen herself has done this for many years, tiptoeing around the bad moods, rewarding the good with extravagant displays of affection. She dotes on him, like a precocious child at her father's knee, habitually babbling endear-ments at a pitch which might equally well convey either adoration or terror.

The soldier-adventurer Cesare Borgia, the hero who inspired (and was, in turn, immortalised by) Machiavelli, was asked by that author whether it was better to be loved by one's people, or feared. His answer was that, if a monarch could not manage both, it was safer (a nice distinction) to be feared. But Ørwendil Hamlet has gone one better than that prince: the Danish king inspires a love that is itself a form of fear; a fear she clings to stubbornly as love.

She loved him at first sight. Before first sight, if the truth be told, for reports of his zeal on the battlefield had preceded him in her acquaintance. He might have seemed an odd choice for the hero of an eighteen-year-old girl's romantic fantasies. He was nearly twice her age, and rough in the manner of a lifelong soldier. But Gertrude's heart had only one desire: more than anything, she wanted to be queen.

No one would ever suspect her ambition, or her intelligence. She giggled and was girlish but always listened more than she spoke. She was the darling in a family of brothers, and she knew how to appear harmless enough in the corner, frowning at her needlework. Many thought she was stupid because she said little, ignoring the fact that, whenever she did speak, she always spoke the truth, without embellishment.

Her betters forgot themselves and spoke freely before her, on matters no one imagined she understood. And there is more useful art learned in young girls' gossips and games than is generally known – such as the ability to hold one's own in one conversation while eavesdropping on another, half a room away.

Through her spying, Gertrude learned the subtleties of Danish politics. The king was old and ill, and she learned that the favourite to succeed him was a nephew, Ørwendil Hamlet, the hero from the wars. It was on him she decided to set her sights; and her goals, once set, were accomplished efficiently, and without undue fuss. They were married before her nineteenth birthday.

Her gamble paid off. When the old king died, Hamlet and his supporters (including several 'military advisers', who arrived to demonstrate their support silently, but fully armed) came to the capital to vie for the throne. But his eventual election may have owed more than he knew to his young bride. She was charming and beautiful, daughter of the old lord chamberlain, and she knew exactly the right words to whisper into prominent ears. Denmark needed a strong leader in these tumultuous times, she said, softening their doubts about Hamlet's soldier's sensibilities. But more than that, Denmark needed a symbol of stability and calm, and

Lady Gertrude had been groomed from birth to be that symbol. She was the polish that smoothed her husband's rough edges. And what's more, it was widely rumoured (she made certain of that) she was already pregnant with an heir.

He would never know or admit it, would laugh even to suspect – but he owed his power all to her.

At the centre of the orchard is a light pavilion, open at the sides. King Hamlet sometimes likes to walk there in the afternoons, or, of recent years, to nap, his couch borne out by eight strong footmen. The court has orders during these hours not to walk in the surrounding gardens, nor to play games on the lawns, lest the noise disturb the king.

But the king is not here; and he will not be there again for weeks or months, perhaps a year. Just yesterday the queen had prayed for Denmark's quick victory – but now, as her nose begins to clear and she breathes the scented air, she hopes the campaign will be long. Until he returns, the castle is hers, and the court is hers. The orchard is hers, and she wants to stand at its centre and feel his absence – the terrifying, delicious emptiness of a world without his shadow hanging over it.

But when she reaches the covered platform, she discovers the king's orchard is not empty after all. Someone is already standing there, at the centre of the world. Someone is already breathing in the air, his arms spread wide as if he wished to embrace all of Elsinore.

A long *twang* echoes through the silence, as somewhere Cupid releases the string of his bow. The fated arrow cuts swiftly through the air, and alerted by its sound – or perhaps by that of the queen's footsteps crunching cherry blossoms – the figure turns.

When she sees his face, the queen grows very pale. She covers her mouth with her hand and looks away. *Not him*, she protests helplessly. *No, anyone but him.*

But the devious blind archer has already prepared another arrow; and even that child of Venus, the knave of hearts, has only the power to cause love, and cannot prevent a love already written in one's destiny. Another *twang* is already resounding through the air.

The man steps forward, recognising her. 'Gertrude,' he says, and he is looking at her as if she will always be the most interesting woman in any room. 'Gertrude,' he says, and the Belle of Elsinore, hearing her name called, shyly raises her eyes.

All at once, it comes: the prayed-for wind, at a speed that suggests it knows it has missed its cue. It chases through the cherry orchard, sending up a scent some interpret as desire, and some interpret as regret, the past tense of desire. It tears petals from blossoms and blossoms from trees, whipping up a blizzard of snow. So even if anyone had been watching from the watch-tower, no one would have seen the queen fall into her husband's brother's arms.

No – not the queen. Not the queen at all. Nor is it the queen who creeps past the Swiss guardsmen snoring in her gallery to tiptoe barefoot through the lobby, down the cold stone stairs, every inch of her alert to each rustle of tapestry. And it is not the queen who catches herself, suddenly shy at his door, and knocks, maidenly soft. No, the queen remains asleep, closeted in her sturdy bed and dreaming dreams of her husband, away at war; while Gertrude, hair down, in her long white nightgown, rises and slips away, as light as a girl, or a ghost.

They lie in his bed as if on a raft upon the sea, and themselves the last two people left in the world, cast away. Claudius tries to woo her for a time with carefully composed poetic entreaties, until she silences him with: 'Less art; more matter.' She is no virgin who needs coercing.

Neither chaste nor sinful, they explore one another's bodies with curious and tentative fingers. He puts his lips against the yellowed marks of the old bruises. She explores his pocks and scars, reading in them a history that is not her husband's: a body born like his, but unlike his entirely. Their coupling is awkward and tender, both less and more than either had imagined it would be. Afterwards, she laughs at the weight of it, lifted.

Afterwards, Claudius is clutched by guilt, the talons of the Furies digging deep into his chest. He remembers his brother and weeps. 'My heart, turned traitor against my blood!' he gasps, pressing a damp cheek into her bosom.

'There, there,' she says. 'What's done is done. No use crying over it now.'

Did men in general take themselves always so seriously, she wonders, or only those in this strange family in which she has found herself entangled? Her husband; her lover; her son – Hamlets all. Each of these men looks at the world through the same eyes, speaks the same neurotic, self-absorbed orations, seals his letters with the same signet ring. Each one more proud, ruthless and stubborn than the last. And each of them she has loved instantly, with aching heart split by the sudden, painful pull of destiny.

Her son was a frail child; as a baby, he had not been expected to live. Not due until July, already too precocious for his own good. A bitter cold morning in a bitter cold spring. Though the fires were stoked to blazing, wine and water both froze in their goblets at the banquet tables. Frost made the air sharp to breathe, even indoors, and servants were sleeping three to a bed, in all their clothes.

The midwife took one look at the tiny, froglike creature the queen had whelped and sent home the woman who had been engaged as wetnurse. 'No use,' she said. 'Better tell them to hire a gravedigger. A pity, too. It would have been a boy.'

'The king's sick for an heir,' the nurse murmured. 'And with the two miscarriages already . . .'

'Well, what do you expect from that skinny little thing? Pretty, sure – but she's not built to bear.'

Gertrude had heard their voices low, behind the door. She struggled to sit up, to look at the child, another failure from her womb. He was tiny, his face no larger than the palm of her hand, but he breathed yet. She drew him into her arms, marvelling that the stomach that had weighed down her body, leaving her swaybacked and cowlike all winter, had yielded a child no heavier than a flower.

He yawned as she picked him up and his tiny eyes blinked open into narrow, glassy slits. They were so pale the pupils could barely be distinguished, a wash of bluish light, like the overcast sky faintly visible outside her window. He would be blind if he lived, the midwife had said, and likely a fool.

He let out a cry – not the robust yell of a healthy newborn, but a soft whimper, as if to protest at his discomfort was, he knew, an unfair demand, since he was considered dead already by so many who knew better. His tiny life was a secret they shared, and she held him to her breast, brushing a nipple against his cheek until he turned and began to nurse, his skinny fists clenching and unclenching, like a cat kneading a cushion.

For days he vacillated between life and death, his tiny body seeming to choose one, then the other. Gertrude hovered, too, between sleep and wakefulness, as if by constant vigilance she could hold his life in place, keep it from slipping away when she turned her head. Diligent, she held him to her breast. 'Live,' she whispered to him. 'Live.'

She did not consult the stars to see whether the hour of his birth had been a lucky one for the country or inauspicious. She visited no oracle to hear whispers of what the future might bring. Blindly, she held him to her body and warmed him with her breath, and blindly, he lived.

On the seventh day, the young dauphin was baptised. His head in the christening cap was no larger than a rose, but there was no longer a question in anyone's mind that the sharp blue eyes could see. They followed every movement warily, as if troubled already by a deep suspicion of the universe.

The king, away at the wars, had left word that the child, if male, should be called Hamlet, like himself. The baptismal name was largely forgotten, lost in the slush of names and titles, real and imagined, which every prince inherits, and which are used, like the heaviest jewelled crowns, only on ceremonial occasions.

The prince himself has always disliked his given name, which seemed to him old-fashioned, in a provincial sort of way. It was always an embarrassment to him, a sign of his mother's inherently frail and credulous mind, and if pressed to explain the initial he would clutch at his codpiece and joke that it stood for his 'Will', whichever stood for it.

But Gertrude knew the truth. She looked into her baby's wizened face and called him Wodan, after the king of the old gods, who had traded an eye to drink from the well of wisdom.

Sophie Orme

Sophie M. Orme was born in December 1981 and grew up in Newbury, Berkshire. She studied English Literature at the University of Warwick before moving to London. *Small Bird* is the first chapter from her forthcoming novel.

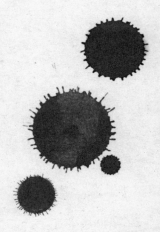

Small Bird

My eyes open. Daniel is propped on one elbow, smiling behind the blur. The faintest shadows rim his lips and that stubborn clump of hair behind his fringe gropes towards the ceiling. He leans over and wraps his arms around my shoulders, pulling my head into his chest. Hunched with fatigue, I roll my whole body into his and bend one leg over his hip, feeling his wiry leg hair against my skin. I kiss him softly, tasting his warm sour breath.

'Helloo . . .' I yawn, rolling back on to my pillow.

He grabs his own pillows, propping them against the wall and then sitting up.

'He's quiet.'

I hum my agreement, scratching sleep from my eyes. It's wonderful. His plan to keep the baby awake as long as possible during the day is paying off. I only left the bed once last night.

He looks at the carpet, searching for the indents where the cot had been. 'I'm not sure about this. We should be keeping him in here.'

I don't answer. For the first time in five days I've managed to have a couple of hours' sleep. It was blissful: fleshy and soft. I still feel glazed in its gentle fuzz. The baby has only been out in the living room since the last feed, but Daniel has to do everything by the book (or at least by the magazine) and has only allowed me to take the cot out at all because he was exhausted and could barely lift his head to object.

I feel him shifting beside me. The bed rocks a little as he swings his feet to the floor.

'Where are you going?'

'Just to check.'

I turn over and watch as he stands and stretches, propping one leg up on the bed and then the other. I watch as his thick calves flex. He has recently started running a football club after school on Fridays. Every Saturday he complains of tightness in his thighs, hot aches running up and down his calves. Now, as he stretches, he lets out the occasional melodramatic gasp or hiss through his teeth. I found it difficult to sympathise when I was waddling around the flat just a week ago, my great round belly weighing me down, pulling my feet to the floor. Even now, I know I am not supportive as I should be and I find myself having to pull back the words which threaten to spring from my tongue. *Don't bloody do it if all you're going to do is moan your head off afterwards.*

I always wonder what he is like in the classroom. He must have to put on a real performance to pass himself off as *Teacher*. Lying half-dozed on the settee sometimes, I imagine him writing instructions on the board and turning to pace the length of the classroom, handing out worksheets, his maroon brogues creasing as his feet bend. A girl with a dirty blonde ponytail falling down her blazered back staring at a compass scratch on the desk, her face hot with blushes, praying for him to pause a moment longer at her desk. Daniel was so easy to fall in love with; all he has to do is turn on those velvet grey eyes, so bottomless and melancholy you have to wrap your arms around him. It's an exquisite trick.

What I can't imagine is Daniel the authority figure, Daniel in charge, controlling a classroom and dealing with the real and cheeky West London kids he talks about after a glass of wine or two. The ones who try to wear him down with their back chat and innuendoes, the ones who sneer at him and call him *Danny-boy*, because they know that only a few short years separate them and the word *Sir* clings bitterly to their tongues. Daniel isn't a strong person; before I became pregnant he would grow tearful at the faintest sign that I might not love him enough; monthly anniversaries I missed, texts I sent without attaching enough kisses. Sometimes I don't understand how he does it – returning to that dilapidated classroom every day, talking with passion about Garibaldi or the Industrial Revolution as the kids rock their tables or flick a beat on their rulers.

He lowers his foot to the floor and does a little jog on the spot, as though testing his legs. Satisfied, finally, he makes as if to leave. I feel a sudden pang of desperation. I don't *want* him to go, not yet.

I wriggle free of the covers and leap across the bed, stretching my arms out to try to grab a piece of him. 'No . . .' I protest and wrap my hands behind his thigh.

He looks down on me and smiles. He rests his palm on my shoulder blade and for a moment I feel baptised, free of the great grey T-shirt which engulfs me, the angry red spots that dot my cheeks and chin, the soreness between my legs and those hot heavy weights in my breasts. I have been unfair to him, I know. I don't deserve him.

'Just ten more minutes?' I plead, feeling the beginnings of tears stinging my eyes.

I move my arms up to encircle his waist and pull him on to me.

'We need flowers really,' I say, scanning the flat. I edge backwards, towards the front door, and try to imagine walking in for the first time. I have spent the last hour and a half trying to transform the apartment according to *House Doctor* or *Trading Up*, those mind-numbing programmes which have swallowed me recently. Step One: reduce clutter (now mainly under the bed in Tesco bags). Step Two: clean. Not having four hours free or a tin of magnolia paint, Step Three is immediately discounted.

I squint, trying to transform the tight walls and wood-effect linoleum, which lies ragged and incomplete at the edges, into a great expanse of space, into polished maple floorboards and high ceilings, into a room which sucks the very daylight from the sky and gorges itself upon it.

My parents are coming for their first real visit since we moved here. My mother did make it for the birth but declined Daniel's offer to stay, instead bustling back home again, claiming to have *a-hundred-and-one-things-to-do* and promising to be back soon.

I turn to Daniel, who is drying a casserole dish, sweeping the chequered towel around and around inside it. 'It would brighten the place up,' I say. I glance at a broken shelf propped up against the wall. '*And* distract the eye.' I mimic a designer, forming an invisible box with my hands and throwing my voice. 'Lilies would be just *perfect*, don't you think?'

He laughs, his nose crinkling, and walks to the window which looks out on to the main road below. It roars with traffic, a siren screaming past every twenty minutes or so. 'I could get some carnations from the garage?'

I smile and walk up behind him, wrapping my arms around his waist and leaning my cheek against his broad back, feeling his cotton T-shirt soft on my skin. I stretch up on to my toes and push my nose into his neck. He smells wonderful.

'Hmm . . . I love that,' he says, leaning back into me, then bending round to kiss my forehead.

I let my arms fall and move away, reaching for the curtains to pull them back further. I stand at the window for a moment; the linen clutched in my fingers, looking out on to the road four storeys below. Although this side is mainly flats and the odd convenience store or takeaway, what stretches before me are a mixture of warehouses and car garages, a petrol station and a post-office depot: a whole line of corrugated iron and plastic blue and yellow signs: Kev's Kars to match the Korner Kebab opposite. Standing so high up, above all this bleakness – unimproved by the dusty autumn sunshine – I feel suffocated. There is a great city filled with opportunities just twenty minutes along the tube: but this is where I am. This is what I have. I let go of the curtains and reach up to open the window. The handle is stiff and unyielding. We rarely open them; the relentless traffic noise just bores over any conversation or television programme. I pull and yank at the handle until my skin is rubbed red beneath it; a great crease dug into my skin.

'Let me do it,' Daniel says, brushing me away.

The handle concedes and the glass is pushed open.

I return to the curtains, running my fingers through to straighten out the creases. A breeze whisks through the window and his kiss burns cool on my forehead. I wipe away at it with the back of my hand.

He scratches his neck. 'Everything looks fine. Don't worry.'

I knew he wouldn't understand. If it were up to him we'd have spent the whole morning leaning over the cot and cooing.

He points to the bedroom door, the casserole dish hanging from his arm. 'She'll be more interested in him.' The baby has been moved again, escaping the cleaning fumes. 'We've got a newborn, they'll know what it's like.'

I snort. 'I doubt that. Mum was probably one of those domestic psychos who had everything under control. Everything bloody perfect.'

He sits on the settee and picks up the baby-name book. *Not now*, I plead silently.

I pick up the dishcloth I discarded. I think that maybe if he sees I'm busy he'll leave me alone. Getting on my hands and knees, still in my grey T-shirt and knickers, I begin to wipe the skirting board, eyeing the filthy crevice between the floorboards and the wall. I've been through three sponges already trying to get it clean. They float in a bowl next to me, blackening the soapy water.

'We should get a mop,' he says.

I wonder what the view of me is like from back there. It's strange. Most of the time I feel remarkably comfortable with Daniel, I know he loves me whatever I look like. But he'll pick up something *light* or *low-carb* at the supermarket and I'll fall into near-hysterics. *It's perfectly normal*, he'll tell me.

I realise what he's just said. A mop. 'No shit, Sherlock!' I cry. I look up over my shoulder grinning and tuck a dangling strand of hair behind my ear.

I see a frown touch his features before they fall back into their usual half-smile. I feel anger crackling through me, blocking the breath inside my throat. I puff it through my nose and glare at him, standing there, still sweeping that towel around the casserole dish.

'Do you not think that might be dry by now?'

He looks at the dish in his hands as though it has just landed there, and shrugs. He walks back into the kitchen. I know what he is thinking: *hormones*. My face burns purple.

Two fire engines roar and screech their way past the traffic outside. So much for the *soundless* triple glazing the sleazy agent promised us when we viewed the place. It did muffle things a bit, but we didn't consider ever having to *open* the windows. Daniel had just stood there grinning inanely, as though this luridly painted, badly finished crawl space was all he'd ever aspired to.

His voice raps through my thoughts. 'I don't know how on earth he sleeps through all of that.' I hear him opening a door in the kitchen and clattering the casserole dish inside.

I picture stooping to open the cupboard. The crockery spilling over in a waterfall of glass, tumbling towards the floor.

The baby wakes in my arms, stretching two fists into the air, his thin fingernails ten milky soap shavings rolling over his fingers. He opens his mouth slowly to let out a cry, his lips expanding into an 'O'. A sharp beam of sunlight plunges through the window, at once shrill and subdued, as though veiled in a pale gauze, and traps us both in a definitive box of light. Startled, he screws his eyes and freezes his throat to block the wail that is emerging. His lips squeeze inwards and he instead utters a whispered coo, delighting in the thin trail of bubbles which trickle to his chin. He rests back and unclenches his fists. Above, the shaft of light grows softer and illuminates sparkling clouds of dust tumbling across the air.

His lower lip unfurls as I gather his body into my fleshy stomach and lean forward, dropping my nipple. I feel a damp tickling as his mouth searches for somewhere to grip and I try to hold myself still. Eventually, he clamps down decisively and begins to suck, his cheeks pumping and ears wiggling. I feel needles shooting through my breast and I suck the air through my teeth. The Health Visitor told me that the pain should disappear within a few days, but it is still as bad as it was at the hospital.

It is a little like when I had my tattoo done, two years ago in Nottingham in that sweaty parlour. That great bearded man, all clad in dated ripped denim, burning colours into my hip. My friend had to hold my legs down to keep me still. My natural reflex was to kick them both out of the way and run howling down the street, clutching a hand to my sizzled skin. At the time it was the worst pain I had ever experienced. Of course, I never imagined that in just two years I would be lying in a hospital bed, my feet slipping in rubbery stirrups as a doctor slid a scalpel between my legs to make a sticky red carpet for the new arrival.

I watch the intent concentration in his sallow features, that quiet glow he exudes now that his body is reconnected with mine.

He was six months old before I knew anything of his existence. Past the lawful cut-off, that unspoken understanding between Daniel and me. And when his secret was exposed he finally seemed willing to declare himself, pushing my belly down and out and showing his contempt for my old way of life by stretching out my tattoo: bloating it beyond its capacity so that lines of fleshy skin cut through it and the picture became strange and distended.

'You'll have to have it removed now,' I remember Daniel remarking cheerfully.

The pain is numbing a little now and I stroke my baby's forehead. His skin is so pale, so thin. I feel as though if I touch him too heavily, it might come off on my fingers. I think about the moment I first held him, that picture-perfect occasion I'd been hearing so much about. I was bolstered up against crackling hospital pillows and Daniel's head was bent just above mine, tears dripping from his chin to fall on to my shoulder and collarbone, running into the dip of my breasts. He could barely speak, just kept opening his mouth and then closing it again. All I could think was: 'Are his feet meant to be that blue?'

Daniel walks into the room and cocks his head to the side slightly, delighting in the maternal scene before him. I reach for the remote control and flick on the television. On the screen a woman shrieks into a microphone.

'Turn it off,' he implores, perching on the settee beside me.

'Have you cleaned the kitchen?'

'Yes,' he says firmly. 'Turn it off. We need to think seriously about names. It's getting ridiculous.' He leans across to snatch the book back from the top of the stereo. He begins to flick through it impatiently.

'I like this band,' I mutter and shuffle closer to him, pushing the operating button on the remote.

He puts his arm around me. 'Come on, we'll put something good on.' He leans over to the stereo and presses play. Velvet violins fill the room.

I smile. 'What's this?'

'One of yours. I thought it would be good for him.'

I suddenly recognise it. It is Mendelssohn's *Hebrides*. I bought the CD when I was struggling with the piece in the University Orchestra. Thanks to the CD, and some serious practice, I kept up and perhaps even sounded okay. I remember the exhilaration as I reached the final few bars, the fingers of my left hand tingling as they formed their shapes on the strings. The warm, woozy smells of wood and resin wrapping themselves around me. In those bars, I felt almost like a *musician*, a real one, not a struggling hack who can barely read music. This CD jars against the remainder of my collection – a mixture of pop and mainstream RnB, the remnants of the youth I've left behind.

The violin tumbles down its ladder of notes before scaling them once more. And then again the same, that inevitable descent before the promised reclaim. I find myself catching a breath, caught up with the sorrowful melody, longing to hear where it will carry me next.

'Names,' Daniel presses, talking loudly to make himself heard over the orchestra.

I lean my head on his shoulder. 'We could still go for Megan!'

He flashes me a sarcastic smile.

I remove my hand and stroke the baby's head again, watching his eyes as they gaze into my breasts. 'Well, we *always* have girls. I don't know where this one came from.'

A single strand of violins play a smooth and exotic melody, throwing brief light into the room.

Daniel frowns, pretending to be concentrating on the page in front of him. 'What about your brother?' he says softly.

The baby unhooks his lips and I lean him back a little before propping him up on my shoulder and beginning to circle his tiny back with my hand. It seems okay to talk about my brother with Daniel, although I would never dare with my parents. In that house he is entirely unmentionable. Unless the police are there.

'Well, yes. He was out of the blue as well, though.'

Daniel humphs. He reaches out his hands. 'Can I do that?'

I pass the baby over, his great skull cradled in my palm. I begin to feel dizzy – the hot orb heavy in my fingers.

The orchestra builds, growing louder and louder and climbing the scale – just to fall away once more into the melancholy refrain.

Daniel puts the book down and takes him. I breathe in and out through my nostrils and my head starts to clear.

'How about Nathan?' he asks, the baby gathered in his arms, leaning against his chest and burping softly.

'Yuech . . .' I pull my T-shirt over my head, pushing my head through the hole and shaking out my hair. 'There was a boy I went to Primary School with called Nathan. One of those who always had crusty snot all around his nose. It would be tempting fate.'

'We have to call him something. It might be nice to have a name before your parents arrive.'

The orchestra skips playfully. Teasing.

'I think that's a long shot.' Exhaustion sweeps through me, I lean over and wrench the book from his fingers. The music builds to a loud descent – 'Can we just fucking *leave* it for now, please?' – and falls away once more, leaving my final few words hanging like over-ripe fruit.

He recoils, flushing. I know I have pushed him too far. He will retreat into himself as he does. I almost expect his ears to grow, just to fall flat against his head. But instead he stands slowly, flicks off the music before its optimistic serenade can establish itself, and takes the baby back to his cot, which is in the living room again now. He bends over and lays him down gently, propping Blue Bear against the corner.

'You should go and have a shower.'

His words waft softly into the air, free from malice. He is too good. There must be something wrong with me.

He watches over the baby for a moment, his back to me, grasping the cot with both hands, his neck bent.

I stand and absent-mindedly run a duster along the top of the television. I throw it back on to the windowsill and stand for a few seconds, contemplating him.

'It'll be fine,' I say eventually, unsure what I mean exactly.

I see Daniel nod briefly. I walk to the bathroom, the silence pounding.

The door opens. I emerge from the bedroom, dressed. Daniel watches as I pull my hair into a ponytail, following my fingers as they pluck the band from around my wrist and then sweep the hair upwards, winding the thong around it deftly. He pulls his eyes away and flicks on the television, filling the room with the thundering squeals of Formula One.

I grimace. He tells me, laughing, that he only watches it to see if they crash. It seems so morbid. I know it isn't that he wishes for death or for pain. But what is it he wants? To bear witness as a car spins away from the track and hurtles towards the barrier, exploding into a ball of flaming metal? Or is it simply the anticipation of disaster which is so thrilling? I don't think I'll ever understand.

I walk into the kitchen to check his handiwork and wonder that I don't have a plastic pinny to wipe my hands on, I've become so like my mother.

'There's still a funny smell in here,' I call, my voice growing louder as I struggle to compete with the TV commentator's sharp nasal voice.

'Always is.' I hear him mutter to himself, rustling through a newspaper, probably searching for the sports section.

I stride back in and finding my hands on my hips, immediately drop them. What *is* that smell anyway? It has been here since we moved in. It is disgusting. Like something dead and rotting.

'You could at least have sprayed some air freshener around or something,' I pick. 'They'll be here soon.'

He snorts, not looking up from his newspaper. 'That stuff smells even worse.'

I scan the room once more, looking for faults, for dust, for anything that Mum might pick out. But there is too much.

I sigh. 'This place is a dump.'

He looks up and lowers the newspaper, his mouth open slightly. 'Well, why are we *here* then?' Irritation chisels his voice.

Here. He means London. Ever since we found out I was pregnant he's been quietly nagging me to up-sticks and move out of the city into some suburban nightmare. He should understand I'm not ready to give up yet. Why should things change more than they already have?

Something catches my eye, tucked behind the table leg, something papery and colourful, like a miniature kite. I cross the room and kneel down, stretching an arm to grasp it. It is stuck fast, but I suddenly know what it is. The lantern.

It is a thing of contention, this plaything: an heirloom passed thoughtfully by an aunt for a child, who was not, after all, a girl. Daniel keeps saying that we should give it to a charity shop, but it is a beautiful little thing. And anyway, what harm can these fairy-tale images do to a newborn? He hovers at *baby* and has not yet found *boy*.

I stand up again, and reaching behind the table, pull it out. The furniture clamours in protest as it drags against the floor. I notice the television growing louder and glance back to see Daniel's arm raised before him, the remote control in his fingers.

I crouch down and catch the lantern, blowing away the dust which sheathes it. I place it on the table. Grasping it, I wind the key: a great flat heart, its silver tube disappearing into the soft brushed cardboard, swept with muted colours; pinkish reds and watered greens. As I release it the twinkle-tonk song begins and the cardboard glows and rotates, throwing its images promenading across the wall.

Daniel flicks off the television. He sinks back into the settee, his heels balanced on the floor, throwing his toes up.

'Can you shut the curtains?' I ask. 'I want to see if this thing really works.'

He says nothing, but rises and then, one-handed, sweeps them across roughly. A thick stripe of daylight remains exposed at one end but immediately the effect is intense, the thin airy ghosts solidified into actual beings. The darkness bringing these characters to life. We watch as the figures parade the room, wrapped in the sweet dusty perfumes of the lantern.

'It doesn't sound right,' he says.

I don't answer. The floating colours captivate me. The happy-ever-afters. I follow Cinderella and then Rapunzel as they dance their frozen dance across the living room, like phantoms circling a haunted swing at the fair, ghosting their shimmering bodies on to the furniture.

'It is lovely, though.'

I sense him approach. He takes my elbows and I stretch a hand back to stroke his face, feeling clammy skin beneath my fingertips.

I glance over my shoulder and see his neck craning. I follow his line of sight and notice that he is not observing the lantern show, but is instead looking over at the corner.

He drops my elbows. He moves towards the cot and slowly bends his head to peer inside. I see him watching for a moment, his mouth open slightly, his forehead puckering. His head sinks further, and I feel myself shrivelling, as though the breath is being sucked from me. His hand drops inside, just visible in the half-light. Through the bars I see the baby's fleshy head. The colours sweep across him, staining his buttermilk grow. My fingers tingle for his soft tucked eyelids, his nectarine skin.

Daniel's hand descends to rest upon his torso.

I yank my eyes away. The figures appear to spin faster, whipping around me in increasing frenzy, their smiles suddenly strange, pumpkin gashes across their glowing faces. Daniel looks at me, his eyes full of horror.

'He's not . . . he isn't . . .' He fumbles. 'Call an ambulance!'

I feel my eyes filling but it is as though something is dragging me down by the ankles. I need to do something. I need to follow what he says. But I can't. I can't. I can't.

'Call an ambulance!' he repeats, screaming now. He sounds muffled. Buried.

He runs past me, a whoosh of air cooling my forehead, coaxing the hair on my forearms.

The bedroom door crashes open and the whole flat reverberates from the blow.

I feel that moment of trickery, of vertigo, of movement without movement, the world tipped from its axis.

And the lantern's staccato chimes fall like swollen raindrops about me.

Rachel Thackray Jones

Rachel Thackray Jones is a freelance editor and writer. She was the recipient of the 2004/05 Random House Fellowship with an excerpt from her novel *No Man Happy*.

Liberty

On her first day alone, Esther does nothing. The church bells chime early, then are silent: there is no service in the evening. She stays in bed, drinking red wine. It falls dark before six. At nine, she gets out of bed to make herself some toast in the kitchen, spreads it with butter, and takes it back to bed.

The note is still propped against the biscuit tin where she left it yesterday. She'd picked it up to read, thinking it was one of Steven's usual polite little missives, telling her where he was and what time of day he'd be back. He sometimes liked to go for a walk.

Yesterday he would have sat there at the table, his forehead firm with concentration, penning the words and then signing at the bottom. He didn't use an envelope. Instead, he wrote her name on the outside of the paper, the 'E' curling and huge, the other letters subdued. And his writing is just like him: seeming bigger, braver than he really is.

The first note he ever sent her bore that same curling 'E' on the envelope, and again inside. 'Meet me at 6 at Waterloo, at the bottom of the escalator outside the Eurostar terminal,' it said. (This was a year ago.) 'I'll explain when I see you. Bring a suitcase and a tooth-brush, and enough underwear for three days. Ps. I love you!'

That note is in her box of precious things, stored flat under a pile of cards that he sent her, one for each day of their engagement.

Corny but enthusiastic. The exclamation mark typical, early on.

Esther calls in sick the next day. It's the start of the working week, and her head aches. Her voice sounds passably rough, but her assistant on the picture desk, Anna, is used to these nine-thirty calls and doesn't ask what's wrong – she'll cover without being asked. Esther says she has a bug and doesn't think she'll be in all week.

Mid-morning, having gone back to bed after her bath, she isn't tired enough to doze and doesn't want to think, or hear voices on the radio. She remembers the weekend paper, and crawls out from

137

the warm folds of the duvet, and pads down the hall. In the end, she hunts all over the flat for it before trying the boxroom, where Steven used to work whenever he brought anything home from the office. Out of habit, her fist is raised to knock at the closed door before she remembers.

He must have been reading it on Saturday, after she'd gone out shopping. The disembowelled newspaper is on the desk, the sports section open on top. She moves it aside to look for the magazine, and sees that he has filled in some of the crossword. Her heart beats. 9-Down: 'ELEPHANT'. 13-Across: 'CONTIGUOUS'. His neat capital letters stare out at her without yielding, as blank as the white spaces left between them.

Steven at the Eurostar terminal, a year ago, still in his suit and tie from the day at work, with a khaki carry-all at his feet which didn't go at all with his outfit. Not the kind of luggage she'd imagined he'd have, but she didn't know him that well then.

Saturday afternoon seems longer ago. A strange effect of time. She'd been in Hennes looking at tops while he was sitting at the kitchen table. Did he hurry to write the note? Something she'd never know. But he would have been serious about it. He was serious about most things.

> I don't know how to tell you I'm leaving, except like this. I don't want to hurt you. I'll be gone by the time you get this – it's best we don't see each other for a while. I've left a cheque to cover the rent. Sorry it didn't work out. Steven.

And a ps, always a ps. 'I've taken a few things that are mine – CDs, etc.' He is so much a ps person that she is expecting the phone to ring any minute, although she doesn't know yet whether she will be dignified, or angry, or even whether she will plead.

Esther bends down to search the bin for torn-up versions, but he has emptied it out and all that remains, at the bottom, are two single stubborn staples. She knows this already. She looked in the bin on Saturday, shortly after she read the note.

And now there is nothing but the note itself, against the biscuit tin.

The next day is Tuesday. Esther hears the men come early for the rubbish, three floors below, and as she's awake, there doesn't seem any point staying in bed by herself, just waiting. It's cold, though, and the morning air on her bare skin makes her shiver as she runs a bath. The hot tap gets stuck and she has to yank it hard to turn it off, but then she gets in and feels the sting of the scalding water almost as a pleasure; the pleasure of penance.

Lying in the water, she thinks of the talks they had in bed, usually beginning with her making a complaint in a voice thin and unsure – querulous, she couldn't help it, not at all like the bolshy self she would normally show the world. Him turning over to sleep or getting up for a glass of water, just to be away.

'I thought I knew what I wanted,' he'd said not long ago. It couldn't have been clearer, but she hadn't seen it. She raises a pruny finger and makes a shallow arc under each eye, feeling the water drip down.

Back in the bedroom the sunrise through the window is gorgeous, and on the horizon aeroplanes are pinpricks of light. The weight is still there, pressing on her chest, and her eyes are heavy, as though she has been crying in the night.

She pulls on her dressing gown. The red tint has vanished from the skyline and the day is smartening itself up for work. Countless commuters are in their bedrooms, the flush of early, sleepy activities wearing off as they leave behind the warmth of the bedclothes. Beneath her, chimney tops and pitches of roofs stand at varying heights. Up here, on the fourth floor, she is the queen of the sky.

If she listens hard, she can almost hear, through the open door, the tap of his wedding ring on enamel as he climbs out of the bath, the mussedness of the towel against his face, head and torso, the more detailed scrubbing of his hair, the slower, careful drying between his legs and under his arms.

The heat of the scalding bath water is still on her skin, but inside she is chilly and there is still this thing in her chest, heavy and solid. At the same time she feels hollow and delicate, blown-out like a balloon, ready to float away if she wasn't weighted down.

The ring keeps her in, it keeps something enclosed and unbroken. She twists it on her finger.

Everything came to a head a week ago. The problem – there isn't a single, specific enough name to describe what it is, exactly – gets between them like sand in a machine, a grittiness that finds its way into every part of their life together.

It came into their marriage unexpectedly. She'd expected to be happy; the marriage itself was so unexpected, the only thing that had ever felt really right.

When they met she was thirty-eight and feeling low. Colin, the man she'd been seeing every Wednesday and Friday afternoon for years, albeit with breaks, had just lately stopped his visits. His wife had found out about the affair and was threatening to tell his children. He had to choose and he wasn't choosing her.

Then she met Steven at a party, late one night, after losing count of her drinks and vomiting in the garden behind a bush. He found her a place to sit and fetched a glass of water. Somehow she hadn't minded, as he'd made her laugh, and after that they discussed digital cameras for hours, both of them closet geeks.

He was younger than her, had been divorced early in his twenties – 'once-bitten twice-shy' was how he put it – and was given to the grand romantic gesture. That first Valentine's, he had sent her a huge bunch of roses wrapped in springy cellophane that wouldn't stay confined to the waste bin. Then the engagement. He'd moved in. Then a beautiful ring, and the cards.

It was his idea to get married.

What she didn't expect from it, the one thing that surprised her, was how the distance between them grew. To everyone else, Steven gives the impression of being open and affable. He can be so warm; but inside he is as cold as ice. He will shrug her off as easily as his coat. It happens these days more often than before.

So last week, she mutinied – decided to play him at his own game. When Anna and Joe told her they were going to the pub after work, she joined them, something she used to do a lot before she was married, in the days when she was happily in the midst of her affair and felt free to live her life, the rest of the time, as she chose.

In the event, it was gone midnight when she stumbled out of the taxi and stood on the gravel trying to pull out money from her purse, the corner of a tenner visible but elusive.

'Mind how you go,' said the taxi driver, but she heard him drive off before she reached the door.

She meant to be quiet, to creep up the communal stairs of the block, unlock their own front door, and get into bed beside Steven. In the morning she'd look a mess but he'd seen her in worse states. Romance was threadbare between them, anyway.

But the zip had broken on her bag. Her keys were in there. She ended up throwing it to the ground in disgust. She kicked it and swore, then whispered softly, *sorry, sorry*. The neighbours in the ground floor flat had kids.

She kicked the bag again and it flopped. She thought about trying to tear open the leather with her nails, but knew she couldn't.

'Bloody hell.' She'd have to wake Steven up.

Going back to the intercom by the door, she pushed the button at the top, jamming her finger on it. There was no response, only a faint sound which was like listening to a sea shell. She pressed the button again, willing the speaker to kick into life.

'Come *on*,' she said.

Unsteadily, she took off her jacket and wrapped it twice around her hand, forming the sleeves into a rough knot. There was a brick on the ground, by the bins; she went and picked it up and held it gingerly in her bare hand, then transferred it to her covered one.

It took her a moment to get her balance again, then she brought it forward in workmanlike fashion, going straight through the glass first time and reaching in through the starburst hole to undo the catch of the door. The brick lay out of reach, a dark shadow on the black-and-white floor of the foyer.

The door clicked open and she stepped inside, treading on glass, which gave her the sensation of squeaking a line with chalk on a board. She stood, catching her breath, and took a few steps forward to the stairwell.

The door to the ground floor flat opened.

Husband and wife, in matching bathrobes. Esther concentrated on ascending the stairs. The woman came out and looked at the shattered glass. Esther remembered she'd left her handbag on the ground, and turned carefully to go back for it.

'What *are* you doing?'

It was the husband, and it seemed as if she had all the time in the world to register his words. They made her giggle.

'It'll be all right in the morning,' she told them.

'Well, clearly it *isn't* all right . . .'

The wife shushed him, *keep your voice down, you'll wake the children*, as Esther retrieved the bag from a puddle. When she came back, the wife was sweeping up glass using a hand brush. The brick was now lying on the door mat.

Esther went up, slowly and steadily. If Steven was out, at least she could sleep on the landing. There was a carpet. She felt so tired; all she wanted was to lie down quietly. Why would Steven be out? It was late. The door to their flat was open.

'Esther?'

He was there in the shadow of the doorway in his thin T-shirt and jeans, hurriedly pulled on, his hair all tousled. She nodded, a movement that made her lurch forward on the stairs. He bounded down to stop her from tumbling.

'What was that smash?'

He helped her up the remaining stairs.

'Tell you in the morning.'

But when they got to the top, the wife was coming up towards them, wielding a dustpan and glaring at Esther.

'This is completely unacceptable. We were about to call the police.'

Steven released her arm and took a couple of steps downwards, leaving Esther to collapse against the door frame and sink gradually to the floor.

The two of them were gone some time. Esther put her head against the wall and closed her eyes. She felt his steps on the carpet when he was a stair away.

'Esther? Why did you break the window? What happened to your keys?'

She opened one eye. He was staring at her.

'Sorry.'

He shook his head.

After he'd unrolled her socks from her feet, and taken her toothbrush, loaded with paste, and guided it to her mouth, and helped her to move it backwards and forwards in the motion of brushing, she lay awake waiting for him to come.

The world continued to revolve. She wanted him to lift the covers and climb into bed beside her. The duvet and pillow remained in the shapes his body had left them, faintly warm where he had been lying half an hour ago. The bedside light was still on.

In the morning, when she came to, she saw by the clock it was past eight. The sofa-bed was out in the living room, the covers and pillows jumbled in a heap.

At the breakfast table, he was already eating.

'Steven. I'm sorry. Shit, I'm sorry, all right, Steven?'

He was finishing his toast and didn't look at her. She was glad.

'You'll be late for work at this rate,' he remarked.

Esther shook her head very gently, trying not to disturb the ache.

'It's all right. I'll get there.'

'I'll get the glass fixed this afternoon. I'm home early from work,' he said. 'Sally and Adam were pretty annoyed.'

'That's kind of you.'

They were speaking like new acquaintances.

'How did you break it?'

'With a brick. It was an accident.'

'With a brick?'

'It was my stupid bag, I couldn't get it open,' she muttered, pouring herself coffee from the jug. 'Where were you, anyway? I buzzed. I thought you were out.'

'Out?' He gave her that look. 'Why would I be out at midnight on a weekday night? Unless I was looking for you, since you didn't let me know where you were.'

'I *said*, I'm sorry. It took longer to get home than I thought.'

'Ever hear of the telephone?'

'All right. But I left my mobile at work.'

Steven got up.

The wife from downstairs, Sally, came up in the middle of the morning while Esther was watching television, and rapped on the door. When Esther opened it, there was a baby in her arms and a little boy behind her on the stairs, and she looked unhappy but determined.

'Look, I'm sorry to be blunt, but I feel I do have to say something.'

'Sorry about last night,' said Esther.

'The hall was a complete mess. Lots of little bits of glass. Jonny and Luke could have cut themselves, easily. I'm surprised they didn't wake up with all the noise you made.'

'I'm sorry,' Esther repeated.

'No, but it really does make me cross, you know. How you live your life is your business, but other people shouldn't have to put up with your drunken behaviour. It's not as if you're young, a child – you're old enough to know what you're doing, aren't you?'

'I suppose I am,' agreed Esther meekly, thinking: bitch.

'I hope I've made our position clear,' she was saying, 'because if this sort of thing happens again, we won't have any choice but to complain to your landlord –'

'Yes, thank you, thank you.'

Her lips were still moving as Esther shut the door and closed her eyes, and still they kept on blaming her, in mid-air, like a Cheshire cat.

She went back into the living room.

'I don't see that it matters,' said a woman on television. 'As long as the child is loved, it makes no difference whether you have it in your twenties, your thirties, your forties, your fifties . . .'

A moth-eaten, faintly recognisable blonde lolling on the couch laughed nervously. 'Well, I hit forty-one last year, and I'm just wondering, if not now, then when? I mean, you know, I've completely given up the idea of meeting the right man, but why *should* I wait any longer when the technology's there?'

The other woman, the host, laughed. 'You've got panicky eggs.'

Esther took a large sip of fizzy liquid, feeling it gurgle through her empty chest. During the day, the weight seemed to turn into a dull ache. She thought of her own daughter who was out there somewhere, growing up in another family. Colin didn't know a thing about her. It had all happened while he was in New York.

She was eight now. If she took after him, she was probably getting quite big.

It's more than a week since the glass incident, four days since she found the note, and for the first time Esther goes out, to Sainsbury's to pick up some basics such as bread and milk, and then, on a whim, to a department store in Regent Street. The flat is getting her down, but it's too cold to be outside for long.

On the upper floor she trails her hand through gossamer chiffons the colours of iced gems. She coaxes out the labels from the cardboard rolls, and reads them to herself. Smoke. Pale violet. Cappuccino. Baby pink.

Next to the chiffons are silk dupions, and then come the sequins and tapestries. One is splendid – the Hunt of Maximilius (1690 original, French) – and a bit further on, the upholstery fabrics start with a line of broad ribbon-striped fabrics in burgundy, ivory, oatmeal. She saves the cashmere throws for last. She marvels at their softness. She has never felt anything so soft in all her life.

Then there are the books to look at. Tiny letters on the inside front cover, a meek green serif on beige. Original prints by John Henry Dearle. The names of the design schemes are a language she aches to learn: slate, indigo, mineral, biscuit, hay; manila, artichoke, privet, forest. Finally it is beyond her. Arbutus. Savernake.

She closes the book. The shop assistants are like fish, invisible to the eye except when one darts out and catches the light. An old lady, bright lipstick gleaming on her withered lips, reaches out a forked hand to slap her little dog for misbehaviour.

A pair of women – a mother and a daughter, by the look of it – stand together fondling wedding silks more possessively than she has ever dared, even when she was choosing her own dress. On the outside, she can come across as hard. But inside, she's the opposite. The women's glance, when it lifts, cuts her like scissors.

'Ouch!' says a glassy voice she has knocked into.

'Sorry,' replies Esther. She enters the lift and feels the doors click shut behind her. It goes down slowly and she becomes aware that a man standing behind her has not stopped smiling. At the bottom it takes a long time to come into position. Finally the doors open.

It's morning again, and she is still in her dream about a coat rack with a lot of hooks for keys, except that there are none to hang up, only her own socks, unfurled from her feet.

Then she dreams of riding a bicycle and for a moment she is screaming silently as the man behind glass hits her and drives on and she rolls over and over on the ground. There are no words, only silence, covering up wreckage like snow.

Through the half-drawn curtains she sees a lit square of window across the way, the reflection of lamplight from inside to out. An early bird. But it's later than she thinks.

Spring snow floats past in pieces, drifting out of the inscrutable sky. Esther puts on her dressing gown, goes to the window and watches the flakes, wanting to catch one. To do this would mean drawing up the stiff window with both hands and letting in the chill as she waits with her palms up, and this seems incommensurate with the pleasure of holding, just for a second, a piece of the sky. The snow is falling sideways now, propelled across the tops of trees.

At last she turns from the window, recalling the increments of adjustment. Both of them explaining what they were doing all the time.

'I'm just going into the bedroom to put the light on.'

'I'm going to clean my teeth now.'

She thinks of how she used to tousle Steven's hair and trace patterns on his skin, those little gestures of ownership; of how he has begun to shrink away under her fingers.

The day has passed without event. Esther sits in her chair by the window with a cup of coffee, watching the planes fly over. The people on the plane have no idea that she is there, they are not seeing her this very second, as she is visualising them in their metal skin.

Perhaps some of them are looking out this very minute through their little plastic windows and saying to each other, 'We're coming into Heathrow.' Her coffee resembles the sky out of an aeroplane: cuts on the surface, lines turning into other kinds of shapes.

Across the street stands a man on a balcony. In the pale darkness his lighter flares orange, but she remains still, as still as a tree, thinking: no one will know I am here, no one will know I am looking. No one will notice me, and that is fine . . .

The man gestures with his hand and turns. He is talking on the phone.

A layer of clouds moves very quickly against another, as if pushed by the wake of the aeroplane. Nearby a blackbird lands like a gymnast on the corner of a roof, its spindle leg intersecting the corner with beautiful precision.

So tiny, yet how it balances. Not even a name beyond a species, and no way of knowing that bird, yet it balances so perfectly, rocking fractionally, and she hears notes and song and even as she hears, she sees that the yellow beak is open now, and shut now, and it is making that exquisite noise and there is no way to communicate with it.

Knowing this, she feels very calm.

At night, Steven sometimes brings her a doubloon of red wine in the bath. She is always tempted to see what will happen if she spills it.

Now that he has gone, she pours out a glass for herself in the kitchen and drinks it to the dregs, then pours another and takes it to the bathroom. Rising from the water, the stem is slim in her hand, her hand cupping the voluptuous bosom of the glass as if she could feel another hand on her own body, beneath the surface. Its delicate neck. The heavy bulb resting on the junction of her thumb.

A fraction of a second, a heartbeat's lack of concentration, is all it takes to overbalance: the wine tips into the water as if pre-ordained, and the glass tumbles too.

In a trance she stares, imagining the wine staining, seeing it blaze dark and rich through water colourless as tears. Instead it dissolves, fragrant, misty, into gauze veils drifting upwards in a wind, the faintest of maroons. When she looks properly, there are no wide ribbons of colour, not one.

Gradually the bath water resumes its level and she grasps the glass and lifts it out. Had the bulb shattered, would there have been a prick of sound, would it have split into thousands of tiny splinters in the water, reflecting, or swimming like fishes?

But it has bounced gently against the edges of the bathtub, squeaking where the rim meets the enamel, remaining as whole as a buoyancy ring, gentle and round.

Such tiredness has come upon her.

The wine is starting to have its effect. A sparrow pauses on the scaffolding outside the window for an instant. Before she can focus, it has gone.

Joe Treasure

Joe Treasure was born in Cheltenham. He was educated at Cheltenham Grammar School and the University of Oxford. He has lived in Monmouth, London and Los Angeles, teaching English and drama. Joe and his wife Leni currently divide their time between Britain and California.

The Male Gaze

What wakes me is the scream. It comes from inside the apartment. I'm sitting at my desk out on the deck. Across the rooftops, towards the ocean, the sky is gathering for another violent sunset. There are other noises not associated with the scream – a passing siren, a door banging somewhere below in the building, wind chimes. From the apartment, though, there's only the scream. No breaking glass, no thud or clatter to indicate a fall. So the damage is probably not physical. Which doesn't stop my heart from pounding. This is the way I seem to be, right now – jumping at every disturbance. Awake half the night, dragging myself through the day. We've been here three weeks – I can't go on calling this jetlag.

At least I've been busy in my sleep. I've filled a hundred and thirty-eight pages with the letter b – must have dozed off with a finger on the keyboard. B for Bloody thing won't write itself. My hand shakes as I drag the cursor, blackening the screen. B for Buggered if I know how else it's going to get written. Perhaps it's time for a drink.

Rebecca's in the bathroom, rubbing at the front of her skirt with a flannel. I stand deferentially in the doorway.

She doesn't raise her head. She just says, 'What are you looking at?'

I've learned not to answer this sort of question. A question like this is a trap. What I'm looking at, of course, is her – my lovely, scary wife – head down, hunched over her scrubbing, an action that twists her torso to the left and raises her left leg so that only the toes are in contact with the floor. The pose puts me in mind of a Degas ballerina, though Rebecca is built on a different scale. Apart from the skirt, she's wearing a bra and a ribbon to hold her hair back and nothing else. Her action emphasizes the muscles in her upper arms and shoulders, the bulk of her thighs. Chunky is the word that comes to mind.

To calm myself, I do my butler impersonation. 'You screamed, Ma'am?'

'Look at this skirt,' she says.

'Very nice. Is it new?'

'Oh for God's sake!'

Chunky is not a euphemism. I don't mean fat, though there is an appealing softness around the waist. And it's not some leering code, either, for . . . I don't know . . . huge-breasted or something. It's just that there's a breadth, a heft, a solidity about her that makes me want to go on looking. I don't say any of this, of course. I've learned not to flirt with this kind of language. You could be dead before you'd adequately explained the various distinctions.

It doesn't help that we've come to the land of thin people. I read somewhere that Americans are getting fatter. Statistics are usually bollocks and this is no exception. *Fat* Americans are getting fatter. But we don't live where the fat people live. Where we live, fat is what comes out of a liposuction pump.

Rebecca has finished with her skirt, and mopped the spilled lotion from the rim of the basin. Now she's attending to her face, massaging cream into the eyelids with smooth symmetrical movements of the hands, outwards from the bridge of the nose to the temples, only the middle and ring fingers touching the skin.

'Please don't,' she says, 'you know I hate it.'

She doesn't like to be looked at, and even with her eyes closed she knows I'm still there. She's working on her wrinkles. She's been talking a lot about wrinkles recently. It's nothing, I tell her, you can hardly see them. And anyway they give your face more character. This doesn't seem to help.

'Can I get you a drink?'

'Don't be ridiculous. Anyway, we don't have time.' She opens one eye. 'Are you going like that?'

'Going where?'

'Bloody hell, David!'

I'm wearing my favourite jumper, darned at the elbows, unravelling at the neck. 'I've been working.'

'I told you about it. It's important. It's on the calendar.'

'Ah, well, if it's on the calendar . . .'

'What's that supposed to mean?'

'They'll all be wearing black, I suppose – dressed to the nines.'

'I should hardly think so, it's a university thing. It'll be academics mostly, art historians and maybe some women's studies people. It's a chance for me to meet the department. Just try not to look so . . .'

'So . . . what?'

'So hopelessly English.'

'I am English. And so are you. They like it that we're English.'

'But you don't have to wear it like a medal.'

English is shorthand, of course, for something or other – stodgy, perhaps, or provincial. English means not having read Foucault.

'I'll change,' I say.

'That'll be the day.' The joke signals a truce.

'It'll be fine, you know, this job – you'll do great. Everyone'll love you. They obviously like what you've published, and they'll find out soon enough what a great teacher you are. By the time your six months is up they'll be begging you to stay . . .'

'Maybe if you'd drive . . .'

'. . . and if they ask, you can tell them you won me in a raffle.'

'I'm not up to this. I feel such a fraud.'

I can't resist her anxiety, the bunched lines on her forehead. I move towards her and put my hands on her shoulders. They tense up then relax. She leans her head back. I like the feel of her weight against me. I lift her hair and kiss her lightly on the nape of the neck.

She hums ambiguously. 'Not now, David,' she says.

'I'll get you a drink.'

'There's that open bottle of red by the cooker.'

I go back to the deck to shut my laptop. Another day of measurable underachievement. Why is this suddenly so hard? It's not as though I've got to astound the academic world. It's just a bloody RE textbook, for godsake. All I've got to do is explain in language accessible to a not very bright fourteen year old the difference between Lent and Ramadan. But everything suddenly feels like shifting ground. Categories keep bleeding into one another.

The sun is sinking towards the ocean. It broadens through the smog into spectacular orange streaks. It's still comfortably warm. There's a clatter down in the alley. An old woman is pulling bottles and cans from one of the bins, piling them into her shopping cart. She's very neat in her work, very orderly – bottles at the back, cans at the front. Nothing wrong with her categories. She's got a piece of string round her waist to hold her jacket together. She moves along the sun-bleached wall to the next bin, past startling splashes of crimson bougainvillea.

I take Rebecca a glass of wine. I reckon I need it more than she does, but since I'm driving I shall have to stay sober. She's in the bedroom, buttoning her blouse. She's put her hair up loosely so that it straggles at the neck and around the ears.

'I'll put it here,' I say, 'on the dressing table.'

'Thanks.'

I take my sweater off and put on a jacket. I find my wallet and my international driver's licence on the table by the door. The car keys are on the bed. I busy myself, shutting windows and rinsing a few things in the sink.

We leave the apartment through the carport and drive on to a dusty side street. At the end of the block we take another turn and are instantly caught up in five lanes of mayhem. We've descended to the city's natural terrain, the roadscape, out of which the squat buildings rise, back into which they might at any moment sink. I read somewhere this city has more cars than people. For all I know, it's got more bloody drivers than people. You meet them, these drivers, moored and car-less, selling shoes, buying fast food, waiting in doctors' offices, and they're not quite themselves, they're on their best behaviour, smiling like the pages of an orthodontist's catalogue. They urge you to have a nice day, to be well, to take care now, and they fix you with the glazed looks of beached fish. But here, down in the roadscape, they relax into murderous aggression. This is one-handed driving – one hand for the wheel and the horn – the other free to juggle the phone and the coffee mug, to turn up the music, to express flashes of rage.

We might have gone to New England, where the trees apparently turn lovely shades of brown and orange this time of year. I could just as well have not written my book there as here.

We pass through a forest of billboards. They advertise TV shows and weight-loss programmes, and Live Nude Girls. There are advertisements in Spanish for lawsuit specialists and instant loans no questions asked. Rebecca's got the map. She's got the print-out of an email message with directions. She's got good ideas on how fast we should go and when we should indicate. We're nerving ourselves for a left-hand turn. Of the five lanes, it's the odd one, the one in the middle, you have to watch. This is where jeeps and SUVs and pick-up trucks and Cadillacs hurtle towards each other. I pull out and find myself playing chicken with a tank. The teenage girl at the wheel is on the phone planning her weekend. I brake sharply, but she's gone without warning, cutting across two lanes of traffic with a squeal of rubber. I wouldn't mind some of that certainty. But I'm too middle-aged to feel immortal. We're stranded for five minutes before I find the gap we need.

And we're on the slip road, at last, crawling up on to the freeway, a sclerotic artery of a city in need of surgery. We begin to inch forward and there's nothing to watch but the darkening sky and the traffic shifting restlessly from lane to lane.

Rebecca hits a button on the dashboard, and we're listening to the polite voices on National Public Radio. There's an embassy building somewhere with a hole in its side and up to seventeen people dead. They call them unconfirmed fatalities. A White House spokesman says enough to make it clear that he has nothing to say. Back in the studio, the newsreader announces a heightened terror alert, and I'm wondering what this information means, if information is what it is, and what we're meant to do with it. Are we expected to pull into the side of the road and crouch at the wheel with our heads in our hands? Should we go home and barricade the windows? The news is terrible, and it's no more than we already know. It's an existential dread alert – the psychic equivalent of a pollen count. Expect people to be freaking out, exhibiting signs of strange, undirected hostility. But we're driving through LA, so what else should we expect?

Once we're back on surface streets, the store signs are in Arabic for a while, then Korean. It's dusk and the lights are coming on. We cross a major junction, and there are men in frock coats and fur hats, and women in headscarves and peasant dresses shepherding children along the pavements. After a while, we stop at a red light and it's Sunset Boulevard, and the neon signs and the floodlit hoardings are screaming fashion at us and movie stars and sex. And Rebecca is explaining who these people are that we're about to meet, these people who are hosting the party. The driver beyond her is playing drums on her steering wheel and tossing her hair – sleek, blonde, shampoo commercial hair – and I'm thinking how perfect she looks, with her even features and her perfect skin and her Porsche, and how lucky I am to have Rebecca, whose skin is comfortably imperfect and who rescued me from solitariness in my fortieth year.

'Which means, in effect, that Gaylord's my head of department,' Rebecca says. 'Max works in television. He makes documentary films. Apparently he's got some series he's been busy with that's about to start, so you could ask him about it if you're stuck for conversation.' She says this because she knows I'm not good at parties, even back in England, and would rather be at home reading a book.

Horns blare from the cars behind the Porsche and I see that it's in the lane for turning right and it isn't turning.

'So they're a gay couple, are they, Max and Gaylord?'

'David, please, please try to remember this, because it really isn't that hard. Gaylord, professor and chair of Art History, is a woman. Max is her husband. If we ever get to this party, it would be nice if you could pretend to recognise them, because they're the people who picked us up from the airport.'

Before I notice that the lights have changed, the Porsche has dodged out ahead of us. I lift my foot off the brake and we lurch forward after it. Then I hit the brake again, because there's a bang and a grinding sound, and the Porsche is moving sideways, dragging an SUV by its front bumper. They turn as they move, the Porsche spinning the SUV around and away from us. All the cars at the intersection seem to be out of alignment with each other, pointing at odd angles. For a moment I sense the arcane order of these movements, as though everything is happening according to local custom and only my surprise is surprising. The SUV has gone into a huddle in the far corner with a gold-tinted Mercedes and a U-Haul van, and the Porsche sits in the road like a discarded cigarette packet. The door opens, and the driver rises unsteadily to her feet. Something is attached to her hair above one ear like a spray of roses, and I see that it's blood. She takes a few steps towards the pavement. Then other people are there, taking hold of her. And the horns begin, or I begin to hear the horns. And my wife, who screams when she drops face cream on her skirt, is gripping my arm and murmuring, 'It's all right, we're all right, everything's all right . . .'

Cars are manoeuvring around us, finding their way past the wrecked vehicles to turn left on to Sunset Boulevard, or accelerating on up the hill. Other cars have begun to move, encroaching on us from either side, and I see that the lights have changed again. I remember more or less how to drive, well enough to shoot us forward out of the flow of the traffic, and we're heading up into the canyon where Max and Gaylord live.

'Are you all right?' Rebecca asks.

'More or less. How about you?'

'Do you think we should have stopped?'

'I don't know. It didn't occur to me.' And I realise that I have thought of all this, if I have thought of it at all, as a foreign cock-up on a foreign road to be sorted out by foreigners. 'There were plenty of people about.'

'Yes, you're probably right.'

I'm still shaking when we reach the house. It's a single-storey building, with alternating panels of glass and wood, and a roof with overhanging eaves. The light from the windows is unobstructed by blinds. I see angular furniture and art objects and vegetation. Max seems excited to see us. He greets me as though I'm an old friend, shouting a version of my name from the hallway.

'Dave! How the hell are you?'

And he pulls me into a bear hug. I am conscious of his ear against mine, of a sharp musky smell, and of my arms rising awkwardly to return his embrace.

'Gaylord will be so excited to see you.'

He releases me and turns to Rebecca. He takes her hands and holds her first at arm's length, as though admiring how much she's grown since they last met. Then she gets the full body treatment.

Gaylord appears. 'We're in the back yard,' she says. 'Help yourself to anything you want.'

She and Max lead us through the open-plan kitchen living room towards the garden. There's more glass than wood on this side of the house, and the distinction between indoors and outdoors seems more provisional. The room is stylish, but looks somehow unlived-in. There are books and journals left open on a coffee table and chess pieces distributed on a board, but none of the artless clutter of ordinary life. You can't imagine anyone here lifting a pile of newspapers off a chair and dumping it on top of the dirty clothes basket so you can sit down.

A guy with the physique of a body-builder approaches with a tray of drinks – white wine and orange juice and sparkling water. As he presents the tray to us, balancing it on one hand, the muscles of his chest and upper arm shift under his shirt. Rebecca takes a glass of wine.

Gaylord's arm is around her shoulder. 'Such pretty earrings,' she says.

I reach for a wine glass, manage to pick it up without toppling the others, and take a few gulps.

Max has gone on ahead, arms wide, to spread the word of our arrival.

'Excuse me,' I say to the body-builder. 'I'm sorry, but I don't suppose you've got anything stronger, have you, by any chance?'

He smiles, and says, 'I'll see what I can do.'

I turn back to speak to Rebecca, but she and Gaylord have moved out into the garden. I see her comfortable figure retreating into a little wilderness of shrubs, where lights shine discreetly from the foliage, and I wonder if the body-builder will find me if I follow her. He's left his tray behind, so I pick up another glass in case he doesn't make it.

'We should talk.' The woman who says this is passing on her way to the garden. I don't realise she means me until she turns her head. A mass of reddish-brown hair sways and settles on her shoulders and I find her eyes on mine. The expression is serious, almost stern. 'Make sure you don't leave too soon.'

'Do I know you?' I ask her. 'I mean, should I remember you from somewhere?'

She shrugs. 'Who knows? An earlier life, maybe?' She smiles, steps lightly into the garden and moves out of sight. She looks about thirty. Perhaps she was a student of mine, longer ago than I can remember. But I don't attract many international students in my line of work, and the hair would be hard to forget.

As soon as I'm outside, I hear Rebecca laughing, and I'm glad she's begun to enjoy herself. I pass an olive tree and there she is, standing with Gaylord, both of them looking towards the pool. There's a young man, sleek and tanned, making his way towards them, holding a glass. He's giving Gaylord a sideways look and his mouth is easing into a smile. And now Gaylord is laughing – a thinner, more brittle laugh, not as earthy as Rebecca's.

'Gaylord,' the young man says, as if the name has a secret meaning. Then he does a similar thing to Rebecca's name, stretching it suggestively. 'You girls look so great.' He starts kissing cheeks, making little noises of pleasure and pain. He looks at them both appraisingly. 'How about a threesome later on?'

'Really, Amir,' Rebecca says, 'you're impossible.'

Gaylord is still laughing. 'I saw you arrive but I had my hands full.'

'Yes, Max said you were dealing with food or children or something.' He gestures languidly, to suggest a longer list of unnecessary preoccupations. Then he notices me. 'You must belong to Rebecca,' he says.

'Yes,' I tell him, 'I'm her entourage.'

'Her entourage!' He savours the word, enjoying its Frenchness, and rewards it with a slow throaty chuckle.

Smiling, Rebecca takes my arm and starts stroking it in a way that looks affectionate but means *Behave*.

'So what's it like for the two of you being so far from civilisation?'

'Do you mean do we miss Tufnell Park?' I don't know why he annoys me except that he's good-looking, in a pampered kind of way, and so superfluously pleased with himself.

'Not one of my haunts, Tufnell Park. Is it far from London? It sounds gloriously leafy.'

'It's fine,' Rebecca says, tightening her grip on my arm, 'but it's great to be here for a change – isn't it, David?' She borrows my wine glass, sips from it, and leaves it on a stone plinth just out of reach.

'Is this a new suit, Amir?' Gaylord is stroking it, down along the narrow lapel and out over the breast pocket.

'Is it too much?'

'It's gorgeous.'

A child runs past me, giggling – a little boy with dark curls and chubby knees. An older girl follows him, reaches out to touch him on the arm, and retreats, breathless with laughter, to rest her head against Rebecca's cushiony hips. The little boy does his monster impersonation, wobbling towards us on tiptoe. The girl starts squealing.

'Now, Laura, it's grown-up time,' Gaylord says. 'Play quietly, you two, or Daddy'll put you to bed.'

The children run off, squabbling noisily about which of them is making the most noise. Rebecca pulls her skirt back down over her thighs.

'So Amir,' Gaylord says, 'who have you been talking to?'

'Your hatchet-faced friend over there seems to think I'm an Arab.' Amir nods towards the group by the pool. 'He was boring me about his trip to Syria.'

'That must be Stu Abelman.'

'Well, Stu Abelman's been on a fact-finding mission to Damascus, apparently. Damascus, I said, that must have been an eye-opening experience. Naturally he missed the joke and assumed he'd found an ally. Then he tried to get me involved in a fund-raiser for the Palestinians. I said I'd contribute to a fund to airlift decent French wine into the West Bank if he thought that would help.'

'I don't believe you said that.'

'Well it might have a civilising effect . . .'

'Amir, you're outrageous,' Rebecca says, unsettled but not outraged.

'What did he say?' Gaylord asks.

'He looked puzzled, thanked me for my interesting suggestion and went off to harangue someone else.'

'Poor Stu. Now you've probably made him uncomfortable. He's a good guy, you know. Does a lot for the ACLU. You only had to tell him you're Iranian – he knows where Iran is.'

'Gaylord, I'd just told him I'm researching Persian art. What do you want me to do, hang a sign round my neck?'

'And how about the red-head?'

'The red-head?'

'Looked like a pretty intense conversation.'

'You saw that?'

'Was it private?'

'Who *is* she?'

'I was going to ask you.'

'It's your party.'

By now we've all located Amir's red-head, who is also my red-head, the woman who thinks we might have met in an earlier life. She's standing with her back to us, listening to an elderly black man with stooping shoulders and a tight frizz of white hair.

'You don't know her, then?' Rebecca asks.

Gaylord shrugs. 'She must have come with someone.'

I'm relieved to see the body-builder walking towards us with the drinks tray. He hands me a glass. Whatever he's put in it, it's nearly full. He tops up Gaylord's wine glass, then Amir's. Rebecca puts a hand over hers, and gives me a look. I console myself with a couple of gulps, as the body-builder moves on towards the pool. It's bourbon, which wouldn't be my first choice, but I feel it doing its job, loosening the knot in my stomach.

'I think she might be a lunatic,' Amir says, 'but entertaining in small doses. She, at least, divined my origins. Obsessed with Islam, unfortunately. Why do people assume I want to talk about religion? Do I look religious?'

'It's probably a recognised condition,' Gaylord says. 'A masochistic thing. Like this fashion among movie stars for the Kabala. There must be a name for the kind of person who's drawn to exclusive faith-systems . . .'

'Fag hag?' Amir says, which is apparently so funny it makes Gaylord snort wine up her nose. This sets Rebecca off. Amir's smile broadens.

And for some reason it bothers me to be part of this. I don't know this woman, but if Amir's laughing at her I'm on her side. 'There's nothing wrong with being interested in religion,' I say. 'It's rather a good thing to be interested in.'

Amir frowns thoughtfully. He starts nodding as though I've said something profound. 'And I hear stoning is great fun,' he says, 'as long as you're not the one being stoned.'

'But hang on a minute . . .' It's taking me a moment to catch up. 'That's hardly fair. I mean, you can find excesses in any religion, and abuses, of course you can. But that doesn't negate all the good things.'

'All the good things.' Amir repeats the phrase slowly, as if probing it for meaning.

'Yes, like, you know . . . tolerance and wisdom and respect for human life . . .'

'Ah, yes,' Amir says, 'Mullah Lite. The trouble is we think we can handle it, but in the end the rage-aholics always get drawn back to the hard stuff.'

Before I can think of an answer to this, before I've worked out exactly what it means, Rebecca asks Amir how his research is going and Gaylord and Amir both laugh, Gaylord more sardonically, which suggests that being a PhD student might not involve doing any actual work in Amir's case. And then they're all talking about the male gaze in seventeenth-century Persian art, which is Amir's subject, apparently.

I wander out among the trees and bushes, following a meandering line of stones. I regret my ponderous intervention. Let these people think what they like – what do I care? It's not as if I know what I think myself most of the time. I step out of the way of the children, who still haven't been put to bed, and cut across a patch of gravel to avoid another cluster of grown-ups making grown-up conversation. There's an area of paving and a table with some food on it, and some glasses and an open bottle. I put down my empty bourbon glass and pour myself a glass of wine. Then I put a piece of celery in my mouth for my teeth to bite on. I find myself at a fence, looking down into the darkness of the canyon. I'm wondering why I let a boy like Amir get up my nose.

Fragments of conversation reach me from different parts of the garden and become one conversation.

'Hey Joel, did you hear this about Schwarzenegger?'

'She was screwed by the ethics committee – two years of research down the tubes.'

'He's a Taurus, right, but he's on the cusp, which really sucks.'

'The way I heard it, De Niro wasn't available so they re-wrote it for De Vito.'

'Give me a break, the guy's a moron.'

'Are you kidding me – Nietzsche was a huge influence.'

'But isn't he a neo-con?'

'She's got a retrospective at the Zuckmeyer – the critics are going crazy.'

There's the gasping laughter of the children, playing their chasing game.

'Do you know the weirdest thing?' This question isn't part of the conversation. There's a woman standing next to me. It's the woman with the hair. It's rust-coloured and unruly, and makes me think of bedsprings.

'I doubt it,' I say.

'See that guy over there.' She points back through the garden toward the pool. The smooth surface of the water seems to glow with its own light. 'Bald guy with a beard.'

'The one who looks like Freud.'

'Hey, you're right, he does look like Freud. Isn't that something!'

'Just add a cigar. He's not a therapist, is he?'

'Hell, no!' She leans towards me to confide her secret, and I can smell her perfume, which is dark and herbal with a trace of lavender, unless the lavender is from somewhere in the garden, or wafting up from the wilderness beyond the fence. 'I have a rule, not to stand next to therapists at parties.'

'That's an unusual rule.'

'I've been felt up by enough therapists to last a couple of lifetimes.'

'At parties?'

'On couches, in parking lots . . . So anyway, the bald guy is smart. You'd like him. A physics professor. There's nothing sexier than a physicist talking physics, don't you think?'

'I never really thought about it.'

'First time I really got relativity – I mean, got it viscerally, like I had a sense of space bending – I was wet. Practically came right there in the car. I was on a date with a guy from MIT.'

'You're right – that is unquestionably the weirdest thing.' I raise my wine glass to my mouth and find that I've emptied it already. The children are squatting by the pool, dropping pebbles into the water. I catch a glimpse of Rebecca and Gaylord with some other people over by the house.

'But I haven't told you yet. It's about electrons. Apparently you can know where an electron is, okay. And you can know how fast it's going. But you can't know both. Isn't that just wild? Turns out it can be anywhere. I mean, just anywhere. One minute, there it is, buzzing about, doing, you know, whatever electrons do – its little sub-atomic thing – Jesus! it could be part of you – part of your ear . . .' She touches my ear experimentally, rubs the lobe between her finger and thumb, as though feeling for an electron. My breathing suddenly feels unnatural, a strange movement of air in and out of my mouth. 'There it is, zipping about in your molecular stuffing, or whatever, and suddenly, zap, it's on the far side of Jupiter. And vice versa. Some electron from . . . God! you know . . . the Amazonian rain forest is suddenly part of your central nervous system.'

'That is surprising, isn't it?'

'It's a percentage thing, of course. The odds aren't great, but, Jesus, the implications are limitless, don't you think?'

'I think I'm beginning to.'

'I mean, for godsake, our neurons are plugged right into the space–time continuum. And people wonder about autistic savants. People are so linear, so three-dimensional. The cosmos is buckled like a pretzel, and they're all trying to cram it into their little Cartesian box. Did you try this dip? It's fat-free. Wow, think about it though. Makes sex seem pretty tame, huh!'

'It certainly is an exciting thought.'

'We're talking total interpenetration on a multi-galactic scale. How do you like that for an orgasm?' She puts a stick of carrot in her mouth. Her nails and lips look purple in the leaf-filtered light. 'You can file that one,' she says through the carrot, 'right under cosmic ecstasy.'

I'm surprised to see the body-builder coming my way with a glass. The ice clinks as he hands it to me. 'Thought you might be ready for another,' he says.

'Thank you,' I say, 'thanks very much.'

'My pleasure,' he says.

The woman with rusty hair laughs. 'Your accent really is the cutest,' she says.

'I've had years of practice.'

'I knew we should talk.'

'Why did you say that?'

'Because you looked interesting.'

'Like Amir.'

'Amir?'

'The Iranian student. Over there, studying Persian art.'

She rolls her eyes. 'Looks can be deceptive. Is that ginger ale?' She takes hold of my drinking hand. 'My God, you're shaking. Are you okay?'

'Yes, absolutely. I'm absolutely fine.'

'You want to talk about it?'

'Not particularly, no.'

She raises the glass to her nose and sniffs. 'Thank God. We're surrounded by recovering alcoholics.'

'I've no intention of recovering,' I say, and take another swig.

She laughs excitedly. 'You're smart. I knew you'd be smart. I'm Astrid.' She holds out her hand.

'David,' I say, 'David Jackson.' She has a firm handshake. The gesture seems oddly formal now that she's fondled my ear.

There's a gust of wind. I feel the cool air on my neck. Astrid's dress, which is blue and billowy, shimmers as it moves. It follows her figure where the wind touches it, gathering elsewhere in generous folds. I swallow a couple of mouthfuls and turn to watch the people grouped under the trees. I recognise Max's expansive gestures, dark against the light from the house.

'It's just that I can't quite take any of this seriously. I keep thinking it's an illusion. Do you think you might possibly be an illusion?'

She laughs. 'Well, sure I am, who isn't?'

'And any minute I'm going to wake up and discover I'm dead, because my body's lying in a mangled heap down there on the road.' I hear myself saying this and I'm startled that this thought has been squatting in my head. I raise my glass and find there's nothing in it.

'Well, you feel like flesh and blood to me, sweetheart,' she says, taking my hand.

'Sorry. We just had a near-miss on our way up the hill. No serious injuries, I don't think.' It's the grinding of metal against metal I can still hear, and metal against tarmac.

'Sounds like the universe just did one of those little bifurcations it's so fond of.' She's standing close to me, holding my hand, looking towards the canyon. And I wonder if it's her perfume or the bourbon that's brought on this feeling of weightlessness. As I watch, the glowing surface of the swimming pool detaches itself and hovers among the trees where the people merge and multiply, and their chatter blurs with the squealing of children. I tell myself I probably shouldn't be doing this, holding hands under the trees with this nicely scented stranger, and I wouldn't if we were in Tufnell Park, but this is another place where normal rules are suspended and people walk away from collisions.

'We just happen to be on this plane,' Astrid says, 'having this conversation. Why shouldn't there be another plane where you didn't make it, and a third one where . . . I don't know . . . you've won the Nobel Peace Prize?' She laughs, and I laugh, and my laughter feels weak and disconnected. 'It's string theory, honey, and you've just gotten hold of one of the strings.'

'And you learned all this from what's his name . . . Freud over there, or . . . the other one.'

'I've dated a lot of physics professors.'

'How nice for the physics professors.'

'As well as a couple of macro-biologists. And this guy who practically invented Chaos Theory – boy, what a control freak he turned out to be. I guess I've always wanted to get up close to where the world is changing.'

'How lovely for the world.'

'It wasn't, of course.'

'Wasn't what?'

'Changing. Not for the better, anyway, that's for sure. Turned out I was looking in the wrong direction. You'd think these ideas would explode in people's heads, and make everything . . . you know . . .'

'Orgasmic?'

'. . . fresh and innocent and new. Instead, everywhere you look they're crawling back into the darkness.'

'I know what you mean.' Strange things are happening at the edges of my vision – a spiralling of lights and the darkness between the lights.

'Which is why I'm getting into Islam.'

'That's a pity, because you won't be able to wear this nice blue dress any more.' I put my hand out to touch the collar, to feel the silky texture of it between my fingers.

'I won't?'

'Not when you're a Muslim.'

'Are you just a little bit drunk?'

'How can you tell?'

'You're so cute, when you're drunk. No one else at this party is drunk.' She turns to face the garden. 'Look at them. All too scared to lose control.'

'You won't be able to get drunk either, not even a little bit, not when you're a Muslim.'

'Honey, I'm not converting. It's research. I'm probably on some CIA list by now, the number of radical Islamic sites I've checked out. Not that I can make much sense out of any of it.' She sighs impatiently. 'I've got so many questions.'

I'm thinking about my desk out on the deck, the tinkling wind chimes, the bright line of distant water between the buildings. Now I'm away from it, writing seems so easy.

'The day they started knocking down the Berlin Wall,' Astrid says, 'I was fourteen. It was my birthday. I thought it was a birthday present from the universe. It was like we were all holding hands, stepping into the sunlight. Now we seem to be in the middle of some kind of psychotic breakdown. And maybe it's something to do with religion, and maybe it isn't, but people are killing each other, so I suppose it has to be about something. Whatever it's about, it makes you want to weep.'

The little girl is chasing her brother round the pool. Their curls light up like halos as they pass the window. 'It's enough,' I say, 'to make the angels weep.'

'No shit.'

'One little paragraph on Ramadan. One little chapter on Islam. Half a dozen questions for class discussion. You wouldn't think that would be beyond me. I sit in front of my laptop, and what comes out? A hundred and thirty-eight pages of drivel. This book is very slowly doing me in.'

'Which book?'

'My book.'

'You're writing a book on Islam?'

'Well, only partly on Islam.'

'Jesus! How synergistic is that!'

'No, no, you don't understand. It's just a textbook . . .'

'I'm bursting with questions and I meet the guy – my God! – who's writing the textbook.'

'I mean, just a key stage three thing.'

'That's a stage of enlightenment, right?'

'No!' I hear laughter across the garden, and the sound of water splashing. 'Well, yes, in a way, I suppose, but not really, to be honest, no.'

'Is it related to Jung? I love Jung.'

The little girl is suddenly still, standing awkwardly by the pool with one finger in her mouth. I'm trying to clear my head, so that I can explain the unimportance of what I'm writing, of what I'm not writing.

'So, Islam. What's the difference between the Sunnis and the Shias, theologically I mean. And tell me about the Wahhabists.'

'The wha . . .?'

'Wahhabists – they're huge in Saudi Arabia.'

I open my mouth, hoping something intelligent will come out. There's a scream and one of the women leaps into the pool.

'Something's happening,' Astrid says.

Water spatters on the stone and against the window. Max is running through the trees.

'We're missing the party.' She pulls me by the hand. 'We'll do lunch.'

I tip towards her and find myself stumbling forward, over gravel, through the shrubs.

'This is going to be so great!'

There's a man kicking his shoes off. It's my friend the body-builder, who brings me drinks. He's about to dive as we reach the stone paving. It makes me warm to this place that even the waiter is not excluded. As he slides into the water, Astrid jumps, whooping with anticipation. I have time to see her blue dress billowing up around her waist. I have time to regret my Englishness, to regret that I must always stand at the edge and watch. But the water, sparkling with fragments of light, is tilting towards me. It throws itself at my face, washing over me with an intimate commotion. The old sounds of shouting and splashing are muted. Twisting in this low-gravity element, I see legs that might be Astrid's legs – green and distorted – and other women's legs, and legs in trousers. I see an arm waving frantically across my face and I see that it's my arm. I break the surface, struggling to breathe. There's a clatter of voices. Through a blear of water, I see my friend the body-builder on his knees, dripping. A woman kneels holding the little girl. There's a blur of shocked faces. The curly-headed boy is lying on his face and the body-builder is pressing on him with his big hands. Only Rebecca is looking at me, shouting something as she pulls her jacket off.

Pat Borthwick

Pat Borthwick was born in Lincoln with much of her upbringing spent on the inland waterways of Britain. She now lives on a farm close to the North York Moors.

Pat trained in fine art, later working in ceramic sculpture before starting to write poetry and short stories. She is the recipient of several Arts Council awards and has been Writer in Residence for a canal, a coalmine, a cabbage and a chalk cliff. She was awarded an International Writers' Hawthornden Fellowship in 2003.

Previous publications include two full-length collections, *Between Clouds and Caves* (Littlewood Arc, 1989) and *Swim* (Mudfog, 2005), four pamphlets (Pharos Press) and three further books (*Chalk Marks, Sheds* and *upshoots*) resulting from her writing with and within rural communities.

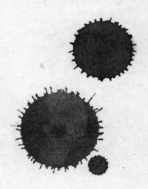

Page 12 From The Handy London Guide (museums)

In The Hunterian

Something I could almost call God
is moving through here, shelf
by glass shelf. Its breath swathes
each of the specimen jars,
settling their contents.
The tall cabinets are full.
A library of strange.
Over here,
the eyelids and eyes of an emu,
a crocodile's heart. They're denied
their rightful last stare, muddy beat.
They are pages part printed. Wet ink.
Then the lungs of a turtle, its kidneys,
the tip of a camel's tongue.
Pale and spread open,
their ghost-wings
are caught in that moment
before upbeat, uplift.
Unfinished books.
Such dreadful beauty
keened from a scalpel.
I learn what you looked like.
Not the nothing they told me
but an eleven week journal
bound in a perfect frame
and published in every language.
They call this the Crystal Room.
If I find where to stand
I can sometimes see a slant light
refract in the glass
and fleetingly bless the exhibits.
I read them
through arcs of colour and tone,
all with a wave speed their own.

Murder

Late on my seventh birthday
my brother murdered somebody
and was asking me, in my pyjamas,
to share and keep his deadly secret.

That night we sat on hessian sacks
in our shadowy allotment shed.
Moonlight slid its tongue
across fork tines and spade shanks.

Upturned terracotta pots
towered on the prick-out bench.
Oil cans occasionally gave off
a metal burp scattering the crawlies.

Still sticky with warm blood
his hands reach for mine,
press something hush-hush
and squelchy-squishy in them.

Eye sockets, he says. *Don't look.*
Let your fingers feel inside.
Eyeballs, he says, swapping them
for something squeezable, moist

but twice as cold. *Teeth. The tongue.*
Piece by piece I hold his slimy crime
and promise a sister's silence.
Then a dumb stump of head.

I know its dome of veinwork, chin,
its wrinkles, cheekbones, twisted nerves.
I know it is our father's. And I know why.
Until the plank door bangs open and

on the jamb hangs his beery profile.
His torch prances across a slatted box
stacked with cut tomatoes, Brussels sprouts,
ten peeled carrots, two kiwis, one courgette,

my brother's hands sparkling with ketchup.

Snake

Just a glimpse of my bare heel or toe,
the slightest movement of my sheet,
would alert a knotted writhe of snakes
lurking in the cave beneath my bed.
Heavy with poison,
they'd be slung between the springs,
coiled around the metal frame
or simply thick in number, camouflaged
among the carpet pattern's twists and turns,
their bifurcated tongues
wavering between needle-teeth and fangs.
They'd strike at the sight of a pale insole
or ankle, better still, a plumper calf.
When my night screams
brought the man married to my mother
he'd cover my mouth
then reticulate his other hand
between my grooves and hollows.
His tongue, strung with saliva,
would engulf and swallow me
as he delivered his shot of venom.

After the ringing in my ears had stopped
I'd fly into a treetop nest and sway there.
Coach whip, copper head, bull snake,
python, diamond back, smooth snake,
cobra, mamba, sidewinder, hoop snake,
house snake, ophidia, serpentes, my mantra.

I've gained their confidence. *Come up*,
I'll say, and then, in their jewelled tuxedos,
watch them stretch across my pillows,
slither below my duvet. Each time
I am surprised how warm they are,
how sleek their polished scales.
Who'd have guessed I'd have them
eating from my hand? I can
even stroke and squeeze them
while they nudge for more, their dewy eye
not fooling me. I've spent years
learning to unhook my jaw, perfect
the toxicity of my digestive juices
so not a single drop's superfluous.
See how much breath I hold
in this single, elongated lung.
See how I've sloughed my childskin.

Visiting Father in the Side Room off the Geriatric Ward and Reading the Notice Above His Sink

Wet hands thoroughly.
Apply liquid stop.
Rub palm to charm.
Fright palm first over left dorsum.
Then left alarm over fighting force dumb.
Harm to harm, fingers in too haste.
Racks of stingers to opposing swarms,
lingus interlocked.
Rotational rubbing of right thumb
clasped in deft spurt
and vice reverse.
Raw painful shoving back and forwards
with clasped lingers of might hand.
In left spawn and twice measure
and worse.
Rinse and withdraw hands.
Apply one pleasure of alcohol rub
using the midweek prescribed
for 10–15 year olds. Remember
to keep nails abort and unseen.
Don't forget
to apply for reconditioning cream.
Don't forget
to leave your gown and loves in the bin
and to keep the door closed.
Wash hands. Wash hands. Wash hands.

Deer

Caught in the sweep of my headlights,
from over the dark queue of hawthorn,
a deer pedals upwards in air
until stars ride her back
and her eye is all moon.
Why she was called from her cover
is only known to herself and the night.

Night Princess in your glittery gown,
please allow me the time, as you
float and freewheel, to open an ash-leaf fan
and pretend to avert my gaze
then chase after sounds
that escape from my throat into the car
while you are the silence of amber and moss.
Then gone.
Reabsorbed.
Among antlers and gloss.
Lost between shadows of trees.
You moved in language I shouldn't have seen,
a script of pale symbols flitting through bushes
then airborne with code secreted in fur.

I know that flowers throw away
only their unwanted perfume,
so the truth has to be
that the glimpse you allowed me
was what you'd already discarded,
did not choose to keep.

Pat Borthwick

Open Night at The Observatory

SATURDAY, SEPTEMBER 21st
The Museum Gardens
7 pm

The sky is smart and polished.
I'm in the queue, eager to reach Saturn.
    There's more in my pockets than I knew:
scarab beads, a Feng Shui pen, a loop of string,
De'Ana's '100 Magic Prayers', Old Moore's,
a chew, a used plaster and something
sharp but at last, I'm through the door
and can see a spiral stair
that will lead me round and up
through the ticking of time clocks,
past the long pendulum and astral charts,
past mahogany and brasswork
to an octagonal platform
with the 4½″ refractor
tilted and extended through the dome
out towards Saturn.
    You, with your Snoopy watch,
are talking numbers
with necklaces of noughts
and now have your fingers over mine
over this knurled wheel,
bringing Saturn into focus
as clear as that cup and saucer
spinning from my mother's hand
the day I told her there was no God.
    You show me how to cup my hands
near the eyepiece and, on a cone of light,
float this planet in them,

this planet, a billion miles away
and as close as you behind me now,
your breath melting its magnetic ice
and mine.

    Saturn's rings cast tight shadows
as does your single one,
its gold, multiplying down the scope
towards a far off single point.

    The point is made.
I rewind home, a long way beyond zero,
knowing I must return you to her,
my hands deep in my pockets,
that wretched rabbit's foot
I should have thrown out long ago,
Saturn still up there
spinning at an impossible angle
    while I'm about to find
the numbers you wrote
on the crumpled bit of paper
near this sticky sweet.

Match

A match is set to a fire; something burns
whose consummate light brings you into view.
Who lit the sun I want to know?
A match is set to a fire but something burns.
Your wife's name glows in smouldering coal
and brands the door to every room.
A match is set to a fire; our unspent hours burn.

Snow

Snow began quietly, like we did.
And then I heard you everywhere.

Up the path, footprints
I'm not exactly proud of.

No doubt it was a long walk
from your car to my door.

For years I promised myself
I'd never let this happen again.

Here it is though, and here's me,
sure of every reason why it should.

Now you've stepped into my life
and when the thaw comes

we both know these tracks
will stay and you will be hurt.

I will be hurt. She will be hurt.
Outside, a sudden blackcap

lands in the centre of my mahonia.
It's found the flower spike

and is stripping petals one by one.
Look, my darling, more snow

and the windows drifting.
Corners, edges under blown white.

As Far As It Goes

Once it feels as though
we've been given all there is,
that this is the most it could ever be,
how can our future
be anything more than memory –
years spent in reminiscence or regret,
an elegant glass of wine perhaps,
a pleasant lawn down to the river,
comings and goings?

We've had our warnings.

Remember last Christmas,
our stolen Champs Elysées
ashock with angel lights.
Then its brightness extinguished;
the trees' sudden lumpy fists
left juggling with the moon.

Another hotel we lied for,
and later, drawing up the blind,
there was no sky, only a pale moth
beating against the pane. No,

we can't risk spoiling what we have
when one more kiss, one more
gravel spin of midnight tyres
could tilt us down a staircase
and leave us broken. Let's settle
for this consummate horizon
and know we can always sleep
to bring each other alight and now.

Late Road Home

Nothing can erase that pale owl
moored on the metal,
the way he turned his bonneted head
to challenge my headlights.
Beak, talons, pole star bright.
A blood-red moon in his full crop.
Then, like the sure hauling of sails
for a long outward passage,
he hauled his quiet featheriness
up and into the encircling night.
Wingbeats as slow, as silent,
as this road home.

Scan

Together we explore my inner landscape on the screen.
He plots a course and charts me frame by frame.
See, here's your pancreas, your spleen, he chats,
and over here, this, the outline of your liver.

I watch my abdomen appear in monochrome.
Ghost-shapes float haloed, flickering like neon-signs.
I expect Apollo to land, a space-suited man step out,
glide strangely slowly across my contours with a flag.

The radiologist has moved his cursor, clicked.
The image on the monitor splits in two.
One half zooms in, zooms in again
to where circles bright as Saturn's rings

cast hard-edged shadows stretching inbetween.
Mare Frigoris, Mare Nubium, Sea of Cold,
Sea of Clouds. *Lacus Aestruum, Oceanus Procellarum*,
Seething Lake and Ocean of Storms.

I kneel behind a crater full of stars
as data ricochets across the void. The spaceman
plants his flag in the spot marked X, leaves moonboot tracks,
like 'cut-here' lines, along my ovarian tract.

That night I'm in the orchard among the apple trees.
The hens have shaken out their duvets in the roots.
I slide my hand under a warmth of breast, find
a perfect egg to hold against the black. Obliterate the moon.

Ward Mouth

The Ward Mouth knows everybody's business.
The Ward Mouth knows all the nurses' names
and all the nurses' boyfriends' names.
The Ward Mouth knows to the minute
when everything should happen –
Breakfast, Coffee, Lunch, Tea Break, Dinner, Night Drink.
It said so on the form.
The Ward Mouth knows *all the little tricks*
like *how the windows open* and *how to change the angle of
    the bed.*
The Ward Mouth knows what all the shifts are called
and that they are all *eight hours long*
except for *Nights* which are *two hours forty minutes longer.*
The Ward Mouth has been on
or knows somebody else who has been on
or knows somebody else who knows somebody else
who has been on every medication in the Drug Book.
She tells the Junior Houseman what he ought to do
and then tells everyone else
she *had to tell the Junior Houseman what to do.*
She can't understand what the Overseas Doctors say.
She announces this to everyone
except the Overseas Doctors.

The Ward Mouth is in the bed next to mine.
She keeps tugging my curtain back,
says it stops her seeing *one end corner of the ward.*
The Ward Mouth can't understand my need for privacy.
She thinks I'm aloof, calls me *Lady Jane* almost behind my
    back.
The Ward Mouth has been in here many times before.
There is not much left of her except her mouth
and, just occasionally, her fearful silence.

Pat Borthwick

The First Moose To Try It

Although the lichen here is plentiful
and exactly the same shade of green
as in the next grazing patch, surely
there's more to being Moose than this?

There's something I've been dreaming of
for generations. I've not discussed it
but have seen in pools and lakes how birds
diverge from sighing treetops into free.

A mountain peak near Vatneström.
A moon with both eyes wide open. Then
stepping off, starssuddentwinkling
andtinklingchandeliers as they fly past.

Rushing wind sings in my horns,
my silky beard streams like a comet's tail,
my frost-tipped hooves pedal through air.
I'm as light as a snowflake.

And I would have kept on going,
perhaps with a swerve to visit Pegasus,
to be near his wise (my family looking up
might have seen Constellation Moose),

if it hadn't been for that yellow car
with double-barrelled guns pointing
through windows at the moon behind me
and two men in moose-fur flap hats, their

one-eyed inane grins closing on me fast.
Back there among the lakes and lichen
there was every reason not to leave
and every different reason why I should.

Patrick Moore Blows a Fuse

All day, way off the Beaufort scale,
the winds have taken vent.
The whole Earth rocks in their wake.
Weather cocks, wind socks, cones
skylark miles above our chimneys.
This island seems swept out to sea,
a Roaring Forties
wrenching out whole forests,
turning gutters into rivers,
the rivers into rush hour waves.
And us, blown or bobbing somewhere.
Of course, the lines are down.

In his domed and rattly house
Patrick Moore, with a wobbling candle,
searches through his cupboards.
He finds boxes of charged particles,
old tins of quarks. His drawers are filled
with faded nebulae and quasars, dead stars.
On the bowed steel shelves, white dwarves.
Everywhere there's dust. Cosmic dust.
It claims the position of things.
Look, beneath Galileo's bust and these books,
a layer of varnished newness, then under here,
the circular base-shape of this astrolabe.

He shuffles in his Glo-Moon slippers.
Nowadays spiral stairs are difficult to climb
although climb he must, to press his eye
against the eyepiece and see neon blues
arc between the fingertips of galaxies,
to watch winds at 1,000 mph scour planets,
to scan for a future comet with his name.

But first to find a screwdriver and fuse,
to mend the plug, its copper wires
frayed and fanned like solar flares.
He's eager for more light years
that might illuminate a vanishing today.

Beech House

The older folk keep to their beds,
their wings tied with muslin.
Through his netted window
my uncle is content to see the moon
open its bright eye. Or is that the sun?
A single snowflake?
Strange, how the snow is so accurate.
Year by year, in a sort of symmetry
it finds and fills his window, only his,
whichever street he's living in.
His grandchildren's children
have built snowmen in the garden
like last month's and down the corridor,
where wheelchairs and zimmers
are parked for the night.
Some have been abandoned,
their owners gone missing.
They'll not get away with it.
Up on the poop deck,
a row of uniforms with telescopes.
They'll sort it out. On his single shelf
there's a biscuit and a meteorite.
And a ship in a bottle painted with stars.
In the bedside drawer, he keeps the Queen
and his medal. And his house keys because
he's *not staying long. Go away*, he shouts,
as they try to untie his bib, *Go away.*
All hands. Up hammocks. Bring my quadrant.
Dead reckoning time. He's bent at the window.
Newton, Copernicus, Einstein, Herschel,
Aristoteles, Hercules, Julius Caesar,
Billy, Hell, Beer, Parrot, Short, Airy. There!
That's where we landed, he says, pointing

to the moon, the sun, a snowflake,
still naming craters. *Such magnificent desolation.*
Outside, the beech trees applaud fidgety stars
and the man at the window counting.
Do you know our module has only one ascent engine?
There is never a second chance.

Pearl and Rogue Go For a Ride

Dec 21st 1960 *A clear night illuminated by the moon.*
Kamanin writes his diary while six cosmonauts,
waiting for the arrival of their suits,
play chess and ping pong in a clearing.
Zhemchuzhina and Zhulka (Pearl and Rogue),
on their long-leads, cock and scent the trees
before polishing the bottom of twin dishes
until they shine like steely moons.
The ones they'll see tomorrow through the glass.

Dec 22nd 1960 05:00 *A fresh snowfall overnight*
and Moscow looks beautiful.
Still no suits but the State Commission
has set the Vostok launch to this day
and authorised the rollout of the booster.
07:00 *Still no suits.*
Two practised sets of paw prints
head towards s/n4 capsule's open hatch.
Pearl and Rogue are wired in side by side,
their preformed snouty helmets
equipped to feed them oxygen through 20G.
They'll have perfect all round vision.
09:00 *Still no suits. It'll have to be mannequins.*
And now, the gyroscopes. The nuts and bolts.
An antenna. Then finally, tumblers
set to 'selector' on Destruct System A.
10:00 *Lift off and clear.*
12:15 *The planned landing time has been and gone.*
We have heard nothing. The recovery forces at Kuybyshev
have heard nothing. Tashkent, nothing.
Back in Moscow six quiet men
unpack newly delivered suits.

Dec 31st 1960 *News! The VVS have the recovery beacon.*
It's in Siberia. Heavy snow. The drive will be difficult.
They'll need to mount horses, then hike or sleigh . . .
to find a parachute splayed across a cratered capsule.
Nearby, a broken mannequin. Through acrid trees,
two dogs in one soldered frame chase chickens
the Collective farmers and their families
brought with them when they saw a scarlet plume
plunge back from near orbit and ran towards it
(fearful it might be God, fearful of thinking that),
a sight The Party, in return for dumb complicity,
promise boiler suits, two cows, a working mule.

Bought Cakes

I

Staring us in the face it was. What
else, with the wagons on the verge
refusing to come up our drive?
March was different,
coming for the ewes.
We were all green then.
Some in lamb
and all them little wet-lambs.
Can't fault the men. I
stayed in the house with Jen,
managed to pull a curtain off its track.
First row we'd had in thirty years
and some game show on the telly,
two families, all teeth
and clapping when they lost.

II

That night in bed,
between long case chimes,
Jen thought she heard a bleat
coming from the orchard.
Looking down we made out
one they must have missed,
a hungry half-day ghost running
round and round the damsons.
I had to dig it deep,
and the flint I used to tap it.
Our bed seemed smaller after that.

III

And then again, two months on,
the feed bins almost empty
and us ready for new Point of Lays.
Despite all our careful phone calls
the transport refused driving through the gates
to take the old girls. Government instructions.
But no one thought to mention them to us.
We'd two thousand would flow into the field
when Sally barked to wake the cock
and Jen rolled up their metal doors.
Like a tidal wave, all combs and clucks
and feathers and Sally somewhere in there.
You could set the clock by it. Then breakfast.

IV

So, as I said, staring me in the face it was. What else?
I'd have to neck them each by hand, starting after dark.
Jason, just back from university, said I spoke too
soft to hear, and was his boiler suit still hung
behind the door? Eleven-hour shifts we worked,
with one hour off, not stopping till three days on
we saw it done. Our hands were raw, our wrists
and arms and backs in a rhythm that let in pain
once it slowed. Jen had to hold the mug to my mouth,
cut up my food, undo my fly and that.

V

Not too long before the stench wormed
from the shed and under all our doors.
Jace on the tractor, Sally on the trailer with him,
Jen, fetching empty paper sacks and rags, me wood,
then down for that drum of sump behind the bales
to cart up to top field. Toppers Feld. Slow.
First time in the lamb barn since.

VI

One match.

VII

Two days before we saw the sky empty of feather ash.
Before that circle cooled. And Sally still not back.

VIII

Jace and I, we don't know what to do.
She's hidden it in the filing cabinet bottom drawer.
Memento Mori. Must be Sal's. It's in an ice-cream box.
Just fits, nose to back of skull. She found it
raking through before we got the digger in.
Won't bury it, like she has her tongue. Gone mute,
won't even wind the clocks or put the kettle on.

IX

Jason's back there and sitting finals now.
The television spills across our knees.
The choice is war, or games
where people wave and laugh a lot.
I read they've unearthed tortoise shells
carved with what might be words,
or attempts at words, from 8,000 years ago,
that today, three-quarters questioned
didn't know the time it took to soft-boil eggs.
That curtain still needs fixing.
We're managing just fine. Getting by.

X

Will that do? Never did like cameras.
Can you turn it off now? An arts programme?
I'm sorry they were only bought cakes.

Doreen King

Doreen King is General Secretary of the British Haiku
Society. She was born in London, holds a PhD in Chemistry
and was awarded the British Technology Prize for Research
at City University. 'On the Edge' was a prize winner in the
Kick Start Poets Open Poetry Competition, 2005.

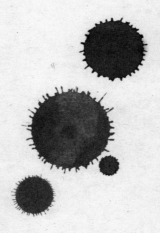

The Chair

Of all the things to come between us it is the chair
and admittedly the one it replaced should have gone
when I found I could no longer rest easy;
when I doused it in wine that wouldn't shift;
when the badly faded corner began to irritate;
when I knew the stained material was beyond redemption.

It was the chair he had torn the belly of once
and emptied from and flung back so hard its arm split;
the chair that was the opposite
of an old friend always there to comfort;
the chair I had finished with but was still using
that every day was like sitting on a sore,
like sitting on a mother of rows for years

and he's reclining with his arms open – waiting
on this new chair he fancied because of its handsome
braided cushions that hug perfectly without slacking.
Of all the chairs this is the one
that because he chose it, could never be right
like the dress he always insists I wear
that strangles from the back of the cupboard.

He has never been the impulsive type and this was far
from a whim to refurbish the house for himself
let alone for a shatter of nerves like me.
Devil red, I say. *Warm and inviting*, he says.
It smells of syrup and wild flowers that should
never be picked, and its colour clashes.

Doreen King

Inedible

I

He regrets giving up his house
and moans again while having lunch.
He goes into detail about what he misses most –
the large sofa, cribbage evenings, growing cabbages –
says his future's been swallowed
then spits out his bone.

II

Dinner over,
having picked our plates clean
it was just as well he left
because there was only the ceramic gaze.

In The Reading Room

I

Seven readers peaceably feast.
They're gorging on marshmallow pages
decorated with piped print
in strawberry books
piled high on wobbly desks.

Their eyes lick detail out of chapters
next to lamps that are the other mouths
opened wide and gaping tungsten.

II

The book I open closes its contents softly
without a bang and puff of dust.
There's only a fine falling back
to something intangible
that smells of nothing
and shines like panes of glass
I can't see through.

The Sea as a Magician

The sea's trying to make him think he can walk on water
and with this in mind it conjures a timeless tide of blue
complete with enamel ships to be picked from pockets of foam

but having sunk to the bottom of a cavern in a desolate place
where unfathomable alternatives churn over
he doesn't feel the earnest tugs at his shirt

so the sea rolls up its many long sleeves with increasing spume
and reaches above the pier's posts until hummingbirds
fly from shifting, spitting ground, but he stares at nothing;

and there's the plethora of white smiles at the top step,
the sea's frazzled fingers filling and refilling while the full bay's
hummingbirds fly at the buoy's tumid belly

dropping feathers as they scatter, stragglers
giving stunned-fish poses in glass air; but he sees nothing
and each aria released spontaneously from the sea's open

black box dies at his ear; and when he walks away the sea
throws up its hundreds and thousands of arms in despair
until the hummingbirds finally slither out of song.

Buttercups

Lustrous gamelan bowls make silent music
to serenade the mother with olive skin, thick sparrow hair
and smile that spreads across the creamy cumulonimbus.
I shall lie in her womb for a while.

Warm November

A routine he bathes in on Mondays
        after they've been all morning
        standing on their toes
        at the window to everything
is taking the grandchildren out.

Following his third heart attack
        he watches the sun harder
        and they wait like children do
        impatiently running the room while
he walks on ground that is glass.

So he gathers them in and takes them out
        to a park, and a swing,
        and a ride via piggy-back, the wind
        blowing from one to the other,
laughter spilling from the cups of hours.

Today he slips an orange from his pocket,
        holds the sun in his palm
        and eases from it the sealed slates
        of light. *More, more*, they shout
and he gives his last segments away.

Bucket of Water

An animal lying low
hidden by the old shed
and bedded by grass
the 'O' still spoken.

I take it up
and out to the light
leaving the exact fit
indent of yellow lawn

and stab a blunt stick
through clear and slime
then probe-scan
for mosquitoes limboing
and whirligigs scattering
like gazelles from a leopard.

On The Edge

She mustn't stand there like she's standing
for her last moment at the cliff's edge
thinking it's the only spot in the world
where she can see a sky that's bluer
than metallic or sea or sapphire or cobalt
because its blue is so beautiful she might
bunch it up like some speedwell
and hold onto the posy;
she mustn't stand there like everything has come
to mean this spot that she knows
like the back of her hand
because she might turn it over any minute;
she mustn't let a gust expose the pink thighs
she shouldn't have let him touch
because now her baby has AIDS;
she mustn't stand there like she's never going
anywhere and never wants to again
because she's been so bad he found someone else
and she isn't pretty enough anyway;
she mustn't think negatively
and long to disappear into herself so that not even she
can get herself back
and she shouldn't keep repeating something
that dies on every gust
and she mustn't stand there like she wants sky
to gather her up and kiss her better;
she mustn't stand there like she's standing
for the last moment at the cliff's edge waiting
for that pain (that will never leave her) to go.

Snow Days – I

What makes it so quiet is that the whole world's
shorn up by a white you can push a feather through
and as I wait for you in evening's bluing light
tiny tumbled jewels that new flakes settle to freeze
as suspended breaths.

Snow Days – II

The sun has turned the snow to mascarpone,
the sky to cauliflower
and cold drinks wait in crystal glasses
for sipping under white blankets
we've warmed.

Snow Days – III

Seemingly insignificant in wind
people drift like seeds into the train
from winter's dark light, backed by weak notes
from blackbirds out in the flesh-picked spinney.

Sitting quietly, spaced evenly on seats
sheltered and warm in glazed compartments
scarves and gloves removed,
shoes watered by umbrella pools,
coats start to open and the voice from the speaker
says to have a good journey
and to avoid crushing the flowers.

Snow Days – IV

Can you still see your father's hair
in the snowfall,
like an undercoat of ash?

Snow Days – V

The day Bedford Square turned white
I put on black boots and went out
to leave some footprints.

Ghostly clouds accumulated
and in my silver jacket I too fluttered.

Snow Days – VI

I wanted the weather to change
I wanted us to take a break
from our separate lives,
to be like snowflakes melting together
but when the weather eventually changed
I froze.

Snow Days – VII

Snow's tears
the sun causes to fall

turn as sharp
as the feathers of white egrets

and somewhere white egrets
have impressed snow

leaving a few feathers
like tears

glistening
in the white of an eye.

Snow Days – VIII

Someone has turned on the snow maker
sent Jodie Foster a blizzard
and in the spotlight
the snow's on fire

Snow Days – IX

I stumble across you
fall flat and am wrapped in a snowy blanket.
How warm is your smile
your hands
like the sun opening a pink bud.

Snow Days – X

It's the longest night of the year
so I light my candle stub.
This poem seems to be about my life.

Snow Days – XI

There seems to be something special
about a sheet wrapped round a woman
stepping from her bed in the morning;
there seems to be something special
about how the white falls softly
like a snowfall blanket
but this time away.

Snow Days – XII

I cannot cope in the paperless office –
this new sheet of early evening moonlit snow
already has my prints.

Snow Days – XIII

The snow makes the day so bright it lights
a memory of when we met on the skiing holiday
and slid down the slope's lily petals to meet at the heart.
I keep a few of those satin petals in my skiing book
and they sometimes turn into sheer drops.

Snow Days – XIV

I'm shovelling again,
trying to etch a path
with big, frivolous statements
in wet boots.

Snow Days – XV

Water has a high dielectric constant,
a high specific heat, a high latent heat of fusion
and evaporation, and as it slips between my fingers
it carries the sun, the stars and the moon.

Snow Days – XVI

The snow in the old nest is like down
on the cold blackbird; or like icing sugar.

Snow Days – XVII

See the soft track
the track that ends by the gate
then goes back to the beginning?
It's where, to greet the postman,
the elderly couple shuffled in slippers.

Snow Days – XVIII

All around is the cool world,
the settled serenity that comes,
(so I'm told) to those who wait
and here am I by the only scraggy tree
blushing in snow.

Snow Days – XIX

Come, let's lock our fingers together and walk
by the lake where so many snowy geese circle
then descend, their honks scattering like shattered
glass in clear air, the whites of their wings swabbing
the lake. Even this grey, heavily-burdened dusk
has something feathery, and when we return home
let's leave the latch undone and the turquoise gate open
while we set the table ready with white plates.

Greylag Geese

Alone and trying to write at a late hour
hearing greylag geese
thoughts migrate back to the day we met by the lake.
How easily they amble by on large flaps.
How quickly and inevitably the sound fades to nothing.

At Snow-Melt

I'm retracing the path and sloshing muck
back down drains, thinking everything else is moving
forward now the ground has softened its ice-heart –
birds revving their voices, clouds in blisters
bursting, releasing mussel blue;
and bushes gaining a green complexity.

Even the corpse that froze and was lost for weeks
ages. But imagine frost backing away, snow
rising, wind inhaling; imagine him alive again.
Today the snow's white light fades at the touch of earth.

winter roses
  those brave warriors
    turning white

Adam O'Riordan

Adam O'Riordan was born in Manchester in 1982. He was educated at Oxford and currently lives in London.

Patrimony

The Germans glide down the spine of the Pennines.
My grandma, cramped in a shelter,
thinks of the lad she met on the High,
her swollen belly, his starched shirts on the line.

The pen gripped in my sea-weary grandpa's hand
bleeds ink onto the blank face of the letter
he can't bring himself to write.
He's too far out, weeks deep into the Atlantic.

Later, as he sweats in the engine room,
under his breath he will list all the Caucasian ports
in which he let himself believe he saw her face;

Belfast, Boston, Newport, New York, Scapa Flow
Spoken into the furnace's coals his words are burned,
substance to the flame that moves the ship.

Adam O'Riordan

Train

Clarissa is sitting too close to me. It's two in the afternoon,
I can smell brandy and nylon working hot skin. We are on the
final service from Manchester to St Pancras. At each station,
wayside and junction there are groups of photographers; as we
pass I see our train run the length of their raised lenses. It is
bright and warm and this loosens our conversation. Clarissa
tells me she was a model. Her gym still has her picture on the
wall; sprayed head to toe in gold but for the patch of back left
exposed. She asks me about myself, asks me to show her
something I've written, offers me a glass and, loud enough for
the carriage to hear, begins to list her failed relationships,
private detectives hired by a jealous husband, the miles of
catwalk, bouts of cancer, the custody battles for her children,
her new life as an escort which brings her to London; *You
don't have to fuck*. At first I'm embarrassed; I might be
thought to be travelling with her or somehow connected to her
work. But then I get bolder, laugh a little louder at her jokes,
which aren't so much jokes as pauses prompting me to laugh, I
begin to side with her, even if it is all bullshit, because I cannot
believe so much bad luck could befall one person. I begin to
think of her as some charming fantasist. Which I figure is
exactly what I am or that somehow it equates to being a
writer. Then she shows me where he put out his cigarettes on
the softest part of her inner arm. At which I fall quiet. In the
late afternoon the sun slams in slats behind her face. We push
south, I'm sun-blind and she's set in gold.

The Long Count

The fighters pitch across the boy's brown face
from a VHS played for the fifth time that day.
Outside a fire-hydrant's cracked, corn-rolled
children laugh, a Pontiac jerks down the Av.
Michael tracks a whole career in an afternoon:

1919. Under the Toledo sun, a branch snaps;
Jack Dempsey's left meets Jess Willard's jaw.
The hands of a ditch digger, lumber cutter,
in '23 a matador with a right cross to the temple
of Luis Firpo, 'The Wild Bull of the Pampas'.

1927. The long count. Gene Tunney's down,
Jack's a junk yard dog straining the leash
but the count can't begin until he's in his corner.
Tunney staggers to his feet and on to win.
Jack's face a peach under the wheels of rolling stock.

Back at the hotel he'll tell Estelle, 'Honey, I forgot to duck.'
The worn tape flickers, crackles, stops.
In the iron-light Mike studies the metamorphosis:
How to buckle his body into the shape of a beast,
bare his teeth, and when broken, bite, taste blood.

Adam O'Riordan

Cheat

As in the beach scene framed on this postcard –
where a jovial uncle is packed into sand
until even his head disappears below ground.
Just so, Ovid tells how the unchaste Vestal Virgins
were shovelled under, quite alive but drowsy,
no longer afraid of the dark or the weight
of the dirt that will drown them.

In this dingy pub cinders in a grate dust over.
I dab the tip of my nose for your odour,
remembering how, like a pontiff wet with balm
when anointing, I sank with the fluke of your hips,
our movements incessant as a distaff and spindle.
Then, with them away and your place empty,
how we changed, stepped up our game and conjured;

two mongrel dogs locked and hot with instinct,
which became a horse the rider moves in time with.
Spent, our bodies two eels fetched up in a bucket.
Night reclaims the light, a bell chimes,
my glass is drained, through the window pane
this interior steadies itself on the street.
I watch the stream of passers-by walk through me.

The Hands of an Apostle

The finger tips and palms come together
To case the prayer they hold inside them
And carry the words a little closer to heaven.
Dürer scratched this attitude of devotion
In lines fine as a banknote, I turn it landscape
And it's one hand bent to break
The surface tension on a font of holy water.
A child's game of church and steeple.
The palms of strangers at a dance.
The convict's greeting through the glass.
The whorls turned away from other flesh
Content themselves with the dull pulse
In the replica they rest against.

Dressing

Up early, the sun barely able to filament the glass
or throw a shadow through the loose casement
that rattled like a freight-car far into our sleep.
You turn on the lamp as if to pen your inner light
knowing what a dim view it would take on such vanity;
Cashmere, Touche Eclat, Clinique,
the rose petal tincture dabbed onto your cheeks;
a restoration-stage rouge which fades
to flush your skin the colour of the October sun.
Our blinds half lowered like eye-lids before a kiss,
as if the room strains to reconstruct you
between the white walls of its memory.
Dressed you leave, holding the sun's gaze
the house articulates you perfectly.

Trawling

The tiniest stress fracture could stop
the satellite that travels like a Trappist,
in silence through the vacuum's detritus;
carbon-carbon, a C116-A solar panel.
But it goes on. We bounce ideas off it,
it spreads the word;

a cloud bank sixty leagues out
from the African republic struggling
with insurgency and pandemic,
the Captain announces they'll fly above it,
a grandmother, cold nose to the porthole,
cannot make out the rocking horse

of the lonely trawler below;
the smell of spilt diesel, fish guts,
blood and brine, gravity in flux,
a coffee cup slides along the galley
its thick dregs are J M W Turner's
Snowstorm: Steamboat off a Harbour's Mouth.

Adam O'Riordan

Chicago

In the moments between evensong and sleep
you will remember how the scent lifted from her
as, blanched in a bed sheet, she left the room;

the kind of trail two parallel mirrors suggest
on any object caught between them and eternity
or the red whip of tail-lights on an empty street.

Or the vast harvest of rye, cut down, trucked
into town to ferment in huge steel vats,
condensed to a shot in a fat glass beaker.

Harriet Thistlethwaite

Harriet Thistlethwaite lives in north London. After taking a degree in History, she worked as an editor in publishing until 1987. She then trained as a psychotherapist, and was in private practice for ten years; also gaining a Masters in Psychoanalytic Studies. She now works as a writing mentor, particularly with students and those in crisis. She has been writing poetry for a few years, and has a special interest in the vicissitudes of creativity.

Paper Theatre

The day the hour changed
from All Saints, ready for All Souls,
and a waiting watching eye.

Through a tiny glass hole
I saw a girl looking straight at me.
She saw nothing though.

She drifted towards a flicking lamp:
horses speeding with the lit-heat,
their legs in a frantic canter.

Paper theatre, dear figures all named,
shoved in from the wings, declaim
passionate tales. Yearning.

Christopher's brown hair had a calf lick.
He knew how to brighten the tiny bulbs:
took her heart with a clover leaf.

Then other things only lights showed:
shadow play when hands grew teeth
beyond the torn white sheet.

Halloween, when that nasty Kathleen
in the tallest witch-hat recited a spell.
Her sister bobbing apples got up as a snake.

Demon dread, stair tread, cloven hoof,
Oh God, he's coming to get us:
she knew of death by tickling.

Mother ever abstracted, making speckled
cut-out cookies, in part to please
her own horned shades.

Moth-made terror. Who was that girl
in the fallen socks? Pale plait child,
phantom swayed. Wondering a lot alone.

Venice 4.30 pm

Mist, yet not the solidity of fog,
enough dulling merely for canals
to be devoid of reflection.

The dome of the Redentore
though grey across Giudecca
is needed to sustain

an energy which that watery
pilgrim view would have fed.
But without elusive sparkle.

Too soon we sense the dark slants
into those dusty old pine
kernels on the lobby plate –

no longer decorative.
The lemon tea is brought
and with it a comfort:

not long now the human
lights will be lit, reflections
surface to erase some deep.

Entranced

Nowhere
    in the midst of the lagoon.
Sun sudden revealed high,
      as ethereal moon-like bulb
    gleaming through cloud white.

Water white, barely horizoned:
      thin line of grey flatness.
Water calm, glisten calm, the slightest
      swirls of current
    undeaden.

Wearily we glide past
    what seems to be
      a temple drowned.

Only three sculpted heads, classical in white stone
    on terracotta frieze
      urging us below;

Not attached
      quite
  to the island.

She Hated Spain

Goya. He got them: his grotesque mad
compatriots in the asylum.

Shrivelled pitiable hysterics, the freakish
and torture-faced sad men;
one does something gross
with another; a woman, breasts loose,
flailing. Unspeakable acts
that presage Guernica.

Death, always lurking, blackens
flesh tints to depths, shadows.
Inquisition thumbscrews and guilt hooks;
closet corrupt antics at court,
overthrow for which the bulls
run rampage on Pamplona plains.

Hauled into trucks to jeers
of crowds lusting gore, their spirits drunk
and soaring. Carmen capes flame
the sword is brandished and cleaves
to gush the life out
of seduced taut hide.

Stench. A hideous stain in pale dust.
She is deeply afraid: the sun
in hot siesta shimmer
warns that the slick-hipped fancy
figure will yet turn suddenly
and strike.

Girls

Anemones in a mint enamel vase,
black eyed and virgin petaled,
are nine, floating clasped together,
on the hall table; attending anyone
with an eye to notice. Such heads.

All uniform white, a hint
of riper cream; thin-waisted and each
has wound her green scarf with
difference, ruff enhancing pale neck;
their faces prepared to meet faces.

Time before long the most blowsy one
will have withered over her prime;
that corner one, greener, on a tortuous
stem may, for some unknown
reason, never open up at all.

Framed

The mirror room looks
so much more
of a piece
than the one I'm in.

The light is different,
deliberated, consistent,
softer, catching aslant
all surfaces in unity;
the books aligned,
tones connect,
calm reflective –
someone careful has
arranged things there.

On the mantel
what is that darker ...?
O, the jewellery box
nearly threw me.

Dunwich

In memory of W. G. Sebald

Between marsh reedbeds and dark
gorse heath, then after
the decaying mill a route through
brown dry ferns and stacked leaves;
white birches, a few
somehow corpsely fallen.

Plod the beach, the signs
'Mind the groynes
Hidden sharp objects':
dragon's teeth against Nazis,
or bits of churches from centuries
lost in rubble, carved faces.

Crude human stumble
across flatland dykes,
mole habitats are overt;
seem to dare watery infill,
while otters, mentioned
on eco-notices, are invisible
but for small footprints
clear along the New Cut.

Sluice's whirl; blustrous chill,
so welcome is the hide,
allowing birdland voyeurs:
the sandpiper's swing-cadence
suddenly nostalgic;
the Marsh Harrier,
hover high, seeing some prey.

Short shift to Sizewell Dome:
huge white awe
like a puffball.

Vellum and Ink

Formally styled
Upper case lower
Serif sans-serif
Uncial half-uncial
Roman Italic
Alphabet marks
In union turn literal

Curve and straight line
Make up touching
Relations form
Intimate fluid
Flourish in scripts
And exquisite
Calligraphy

Salford

Everything clean edged. Straight:
stone, glass, concrete, metal;
that ice-bite wind seeking to scour
through canyon quays chills
our bones, no gloves or hats.

We look shining War Museum:
no altering the numb within, even
the lily-valley wedding photo beside
1918 release book is only bell-
distant haunt of sadly warmer.

The high lookout box tower,
through bars, is hell stirring:
sudden sight of 'forty-four and drop
down the steel grill
beneath our small feet.

We emerge relieved that's done;
with daunted thoughts
of the slog way back:
people scarce, only accidental
grass for colour.

Then up against grey, a large bird: black, long-necked,
at first ungainly, then shooting
forward its long-oval
body weights a purpose
vital.

Cormorant.

Free of the drawing board
it carries heart.

Breath Lessons

I remember whooping cough.

Late sun slant through
the window lit that felted
mat with its fawn and bird
for years on bathroom floor.

The room hung
high in the house
buttressed, way out over the garden –
precipitous.

No one came, dread worse:
I retched, whooping,
hunch shouldered,
thread-thin sense of last

day here. Solo
conquerer of the next bout:
a rite passage to sturdy
the small frame –

stare out the window,
a swan flies up from the college
pond – ready me for
the far and farther.

Teazel

Sharp and tall above,
stands isolate dour; head –
higher than sog chrysanthemums,
worse for winter frost fast –

bristles out of nut-shade bulb;

shameless whiskers shoulder girdle
awkward reaching to brittle stem
appears quite naked cold –
secret seeds inside.

Inside tough cranium helmet
our beige globular brain –
such unneutral neural word
making visceral machine of us –

has driven dread-joy route here.

One view of the invisible
circuit mystery, fuelled by
force twined in patterns past –
something's missing.

Riddle

' ... *who, with trickling increment,*
Veins violets and tall trees makes more and more'
Hopkins

Colossal energy and spirit sent
me on a climb for long stare at trickling:
just the seduce of its swift emollience
over stones, in the depth of stream sparkling,
whose very lift has shoaled each present.
Added rain begins its fecund sprinkling –
once essence poised as vaporous cloud –
and casts its own musical dib-dab-spots.
What tumbles and twists with the current goad,
is play fleeting over-n-under rocks
in a rush to shift-swaddle the next bed
full of swirl-fish weed species, and cascade
over grand slabs of Welsh granite and slate
where I clutch a lichened branch at my head.

Adele Ward

Adele Ward lives in north-west London with her two sons, Stefano and Daniel. She worked as a journalist and author of non-fiction before spending four years in Italy where her children were born. She has a BA in English and American Literature from the University of Kent and an MA in Literature from the Open University.

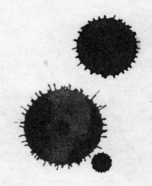

Pen Llŷn

We hurried on,
past the washed-out sign
with its painted finger pointing
TO THE BEACH.
Expectant, seeing only bees
hover in the wild broom's glow,
shouldering the lane narrow.

Over a ridge we found the sea,
caught in the glare of a white sunrise:
desolate except for gulls
and one windswept walker,
whose dog circled then
flung itself at the sea
as she hurled a javelin stick.

At our laughter's echo
they mounted the far path,
diminishing along the cliff's edge
that winds towards Pwllheli.
The cove, a primitive confessional,
demanded each must approach in turn.
Our entry banished her.

To our other side, sheer rock
where the sea crashed foam
house high, while at our feet
harmless waves lapped feebly
at worm casts. Land enclosed us —
even on the sea's horizon
shadow mountains curved
completing Tremadog Bay.

I'd taken worry but left it
there, absorbed by stones.
And wondered what passed
between my sons' palms
and the pebbles they chose with care
to toss, watchful, into the sea.
Or the rocks they heaved between them
to unburden into pools.

Wordlessly they planted
stones tilting up, in circles
like nests of dinosaur eggs.
Then searched for crabs
or starfish, finding only
empty mussel shells, a tangled
fishing net, a branch
licked white and smooth
as a femur lacking its skeleton.

They brought away two rocks,
large as my hands: one grey,
one pink and blue – veined
like a newborn's transparent skin.
When I hold them to my cheeks
the cold seeps through
and remains like a taste in my mouth.

Better than a conch it summons up
the bite and smell of the wind
from a slate blue sea;
a lone figure vanishing on the cliff;
the pained yelp of the gulls.

La Casa al Mare
(Metaponto, Italy)

I

Not an insect click, not a bird
chirrup. Italian midday heat
stilled life.

I was bare and breastfeeding,
perched on the bed's edge:
solid as carved stone,
if marble could trickle sweat
at each moulded point
where plump limbs adhere.

Against my calves a white sheet
draped to the ground. In front
the jammed window yawned.
No breeze entered:
only the scent of pine woods
arrived and hung stickily.

The crisp sheet rippled in
motionless air. A curved shape
moved in the under-mattress shade
stroking my ankles.
My dog, I thought, jealous
perhaps of the child, perhaps
smelling the sweet milk.
I would have reached

under to touch his fur,
but my son swayed
in drooping headed sleep.
The glistening shellfish
whorl of his mouth
contracted, suckling air.
I gathered him to me and lay
back, my feet sliding
to cooler tiles. And slept.

II

            Then woke
to the crackling of a cicada
crashing from wall
to white wall. Chasing light.
My starfish son still spread,
oblivious, freefalling through sleep.
So I rose and leaned
both arms heavily on the sill.

There was my husband,
arms full of pine cones,
stooping to line them up
where the sun could woo them,
tease them open to offer us
gluey *pinoli*.
Beside him the panting dog
I'd believed was with me.

III

The ridge between window
and shutter was lined with skin:
like human calluses,
like years of clipped nails
accumulated.
Another mother had claimed this house
before us: had slept with us and her young,
in the room with her favoured shade.

She had touched me
as I now almost
touched her: my folded arms
mirroring the full length
of muscular twist and tangle –
the zigzagged grey and black
that were code for viper and lethal.

La Casa al Mare – holiday home by the sea
Pinoli – pine kernels

Eclipse

At the time of the last solar eclipse
    we were still together.

They were selling viewers in Tesco's,
    one pound a pair, so I bought two.

You wasted your money, my husband said.
    He'd already bought his.

When the countdown started
    both my pairs were lost –

so I stood in the garden watching my husband
    watching the eclipse.

He said it was disappointing.

Eels

At Canterbury's Westgate
we dawdled on the riverbank
feeding fried chicken skins
to pestering eels.
The shallow Stour
writhed black with coils
weaving around us
binding our ankles.
Their lamprey mouths
suctioned toes
like infant gums
leeching nipples.
Needle-sharp teeth
shocked, injecting
electric thrills
up through my spine.
We couldn't resist
plunging bare feet
into the plait
of slithering muscles.
In those days we were
as thin as eels
and as hungry.

Solid Wood

Our first table still stands
in a corner at my parents' house
covered in box-files.

It was with us from our first bedsit
until the day we chose separate homes.
I wanted it for my portable

typewriter, and so we could have
proper dinners. You found it
in a secondhand ad

and we walked miles to see it.
The owner had placed daffodils
in the centre, to bring out

its golden grain. I loved it
straight away – the spiralling legs
and smoothness wanting to be stroked.

'We'll take it,' I said, 'we can carry it.'
Then she raised a hand to her stiff hair
saying, 'It's not possible.'

She was excited, though,
to think her table could float
through the door and sail

down winding Canterbury streets,
buoyed up on the shoulders
of determined teenagers.

Herne Bay

I always wanted to live by the sea
but not this sea with its sewage smell,
its bed of greased stones
and green slime waiting to web toes.

This was a sea I needed to escape.
Instead the thrash of waves gave no reprieve,
while endless orchestras of seagull shrieks
clashed pitiless on all sides.

I sat in the only soundproof, windowless
refuge for hours – until my head
echoed the torture of water and gulls,
pounding me from inside.

So we set out on walks, confronting the sea
head on. Past the high wall
of the convent, where smoke
rose night and day from the yard.

One day we spotted them, paddling –
shell-coloured habits raised and tucked
like pantaloons, clutched by hands
that were shining and pink as claws.

Wind billowed the folds, loose cloth
tugged backwards from their shoulders
in jagged wings. They were together
but separate, a ragged V

of seabirds trying to land in a storm.
Bare faces angled back and up,
glistening, framed in cowls.
Their laughter shrieked, abandoned.

Midnight Swim

Whitstable was the place to be.
While our hot newspapers bulged
with hake and pea fritters
they feasted on oysters.

Once we warmed ourselves at their hearth
with real ale, until someone shouted *Skinny dip!*
and we were jostled out, unbelieving,
snaking through upturned boats on the winter beach.

They stripped off in unison and hobbled
off down the sheer, pebble-sharp slope,
arms and legs scissored outwards and buttocks
clenched, like a line of Lawrentian heroes.

They looked set for France, wading in until
the sea reached the bollock line and they froze,
then charged out with a scream. Back up the shore,
almost on all fours, clambering to where we sat

throwing pebbles that sparked like embers
bouncing seawards. The same voice called
New game! and they all forgot cold or clothes
to scramble for handfuls of stones; then turned,

hurling them harder and faster, racing
to keep the scattered sparks alight,
igniting frenzied laughter we couldn't stop
until the whole beach was on fire.

The Last Time I Wore Fur

It was genuine musquash, tracked down
in a wardrobe at my mother's house,
hiding beneath dead relatives' spoils.

I unearthed it, curled like an animal
hibernating: cold to the touch
when I lifted it by the arm.

Its cool embrace enclosed
and slithered against me –
a weighty second skin

that protected me from winter.
Even the sea wind couldn't
penetrate. Fear rolled off like rain.

Framed in its raised collar I was
glamorous as Ava Gardner,
powerful as Henry the Eighth.

My musquash coat could go
anywhere, and took me with it.
Doors opened but no tigers leaped.

Until spring when it needed shaded sleep –
and I, with my freshly shed skin,
was naked and tender as a grass snake.

One June day, desperate for winter,
I opened the cupboard door where it rested.
Disturbed, the fur twitched, alive.

Adele Ward

At my touch its front
split open like a wound
with pustular larvae

squirming in the sun.
Then amber and dust-coloured moths
scattered like ash in my face.

In Silence

The only way to be with him
was to join him
at dawn on the riverbank,
threading maggots with hooks,
casting out,
eyeing the float until it bobbed

under and that smug feeling
at getting the first bite.
A quick flick upwards
to pierce an armoured lip,
and the victor's joy of watching
a fish winched into captivity.

Then waiting as careful hands
cradled my catch.
'It's swallowed the hook.'
He should have killed it then
but he always threw fish back
so he eased the hook out slowly,
tearing against tissue,

and all the time I was watching
feeling the hook in my stomach.
Until he stooped and handed the fish
to the water. It turned tail and left –
a thin red wake twisting behind
rising in sudden petals.

Adele Ward

Source

It was taken one mild Easter
in Munich, which explains
my thin ochre dress and black patent shoes.

We drove to the Black Forest –
though I didn't know the destination.
High on the mountain

the others pulled out coats and boots,
then set off lagged and laughing
at the ridiculous English.

Up there the snow was knee deep –
they said I could wait in the car.
Instead I went with them,

threading my feet into the deep
broad bootprints of the tallest man –
as a child might learn to sew

following patterned holes cut in cardboard.
My shoes left no evidence; my legs
never touched the snow. I wasn't really there.

It didn't even feel cold. I concentrated
so hard on walking I couldn't see the Danube
until I nearly stepped in it.

Foxgloves

This autumn I will plant
foxgloves. I have had my fill
of the sweetness of roses, the
intoxication of honeysuckle
and the calm of white lilac.

Foxgloves, I thought, were wild
but here they are packeted:
the purple, the pink, the white,
with scarlet-speckled throats.

I long to see their blades
cut through borders, raise
beckoning fingers five feet high.

Here I am, armed with a hundred seeds.
I will fill my garden with venom
this autumn. Nothing else will do.

Cymbidium

That was the first time I saw orchids.

A neighbour called over the hedge
though he didn't like children.
Being twelve I obeyed,
even if his mouth was too
old man voluptuous.
Glaucous eyes behind
thick lenses caught and held me captive.

I followed
into a dark back room
where his wife sat in the corner,
so still she might have been dead,
then stepped around

        his special door
into the warm extension.
The walls were glazed –
light filtered wetly
through overlapping fronds.
Flowers perched like fine curled
slices of moist raw veal.

He showed me his pride: cymbidium orchids –

See how they grip the climbers:
they live on trees,
sucking up water and leaf litter
as it drips down the bark.

Epiphytic, he called them.
Parasites, I thought.

Hold out your hands.

He sliced off an orchid head –
planted it, corpse cool,
in my upturned palms.
I held it: stemless, wounded,
incapable of survival.
Nothing but a gaping mouth –
amputated, silent.

Then he took a hooked knife,
cut away clinging roots
and tore through, as if
parting curtains.

Look. That's where I watch you play.

From his hide I peered
into my own clearing: a square of lawn –
sunlight painful after the shade.
My own discarded tennis racket waiting.

Cookham Horses

The horsey girls rode past each day –
square in the saddle, backs straight,
while I craved a cream-coloured horse,
a wine-red riding jacket.
So I raced my bike
at a gallop up Bradcutts Lane
to straddle the fence at the paddocks
where horses ran free.

My favourite ambled over,
raised a velvet muzzle to my nose
and we breathed each other's breath,
exchanging lung scents.
Then rested heavily on my shoulder,
beard-coarse hair stroking my cheek.

Until the horsey girls surprised us,
blonde hair gleaming anger from rigid plaits.
Their jealous rage was sparks off flint
from glassy eyes and polished boots.
They would have liked to whip me
with the curved tan leather
of their fist-clenched riding crops.

But I bowed before them,
shamed by their ownership,
as a circus-horse humbly
kneels, its head lowered,
or awkwardly paws the ground.
While the horse gambolled off
with a flourish of carousel tail,
the joy of a bare back and a kick
of both rear hooves
at us and into the sky.

Advice To Women From A Spinster With Dog

My words are true although I speak in jest:
when looking for a friend to share your days
of men or dogs you'll find that dogs are best.

You may be ugly, old or badly dressed –
your dog will watch you with a loving gaze.
My words are true although I speak in jest.

No dog would ever put you to the test:
the worst cooked meal will always win his praise.
Of men or dogs you'll find that dogs are best.

At giving love, and taking, dogs are blessed
with expertise – affection is their craze.
My words are true although I speak in jest.

And if you find your dog has too much zest
for females, ask the vet to change his ways.
Of men or dogs you'll find that dogs are best.

Then with your chosen canine you can rest
assured of lifelong love that never strays.
My words are true although I speak in jest:
of men or dogs you'll find that dogs are best.

(This poem was read on Radio 3 by Wendy Cope when it won The Verb
Villanelle Competition)

J. T. Welsch

J. T. Welsch is from near St. Louis.

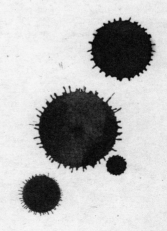

A Truth for Thomas

My oldest asked me just last week whether –
   as some only child type of smart-aleck
had informed him – dinosaurs had feathers.

Pinky-swearing otherwise, I proffered a knee,
   & enlightened him as to the catfish
the size of old Buicks that sleep beneath

the dam & just keep growing, God knows how long.
   Granted, I needn't have added that I've
met divers who went down looking for something

else & found them with their scuba flashlights –
   big enough to swallow them whole alive –
but I did & thus endures the kind, fine line

   betwixt imaginations & a lie.

J. T. Welsch

Bucolica Temporalis

James St. runs to this field
where I'll cut left, side-step
the wet sunken trench with pieces
of old snow then back toward the break
in the row of remaining
poplars where I can cross
that new state bypass to the cornfields
on the north side, see all
the ragged little stumps belonging
to an old friend of mine's family
who'd spot my red ballcap once
they glance out a window, so I'll hurry
through the Indian grass, man high, nicking
my face, closing my mouth, certain
I haven't had cockaburrs
in ages, but my sleeves
& pantslegs are filled with them
when I've made it to Moore Road, not
the straightest but most practical route,
picking up the noise of the backhoe
I saw yesterday morning digging by
the fuel tanks across from the Schewe farm –
(always dragging this sensation of *time*
something like the air
temperature against my body's or the sky
being blue enough & feeling the weak low sun
upon my back, seeing no clouds)
& just one thin trail of smoke
from what must be another farmhouse chimney,
off a good few miles yet.

Bluegill

Papa picked me
up, this was after he retired & sold
his fat little boat with the green bottom.
First, we went by the garage. Cosmo strolled
out from
the back in his dirty

coveralls & while Papa joked
with the young
salesguy they let me sit
in the new Mustang[1]
just come in. One last stop for crickets,
then we drove out to Luhr's lake

by the Country Club,
& the White Rat[2] himself was
there –
out on the water with Alois!
Papa said he knew they were
friends. They waved back at us.

After we got
a chain's worth, I guess, we
went back & showed
Grammy
what I caught & she made me a bowl
of sherbet & we sat

on a cooler to watch
Papa clean them in the driveway, making
a pile
of guts on a newspaper. Just that spring
at school we'd voted bluegill
the new state fish.[3]

---

[1] A popular, relatively low-priced sports car manufactured by Ford since
mid-1964 when 22,000 were sold on their first day available.
[2] Whitey Herzog, general manager of the Kansas City Royals (1975–9),
and the St Louis Cardinals (1980–90), leading both teams to three
pennants each and securing a World Series victory for the Cardinals in
1982. He was a player in the majors as well, from 1956 to 1963.
[3] In 1986, Illinois schoolchildren indeed 'elected' *Lepomis macrochirus*
their first State Fish.

In Western Kansas

one:

The first police car came suddenly,
quickly from behind, pulled in ahead
meaning to slow everyone down,
but also made us concerned.

The second one appeared a minute
later, coming from ahead, down the shoulder
in the wrong direction, leading a red semi
pulling a livestock-hauler.

The trailer's holes were dark,
I saw, passing in opposite directions.
Just then, I did wonder if any animals
might have been hurt.

Our own escort slowed us further
& held us aside in the left lane
     as we approached.

two:

There were two or three more police cars.
Every one of them with lights, but no sirens.

However slow we were going, it seemed to fly past.
One was pointed towards us, parked on the shoulder,
again in the wrong direction.

The other two were in that empty right lane,
directing us around.

I remember one policeman's face:
he wore sunglasses. It was a bright, clear day.

He was facing us & waved his arm
to just continue along.

'Gawking at accidents is what makes for
such awful traffic, you sick bastards,'
I said to myself aloud.

three:

I'd seen the second big truck as we approached,
but couldn't see till a gap between
two of the cop's cars –

two dark bodies were jammed together
behind & beneath this other truck's rear wheel.

Who knows if there were others,
or how many, inside or back where I couldn't see?

(Maybe that first truck that passed
was carrying away frightened survivors.)

One of their dead faces was showing:

her head lay back on its side on the pavement,
her mouth was slightly open,
but her one eye that I could see was closed.

(I wonder if someone shut it.)

four:

That was all I saw in the
two seconds driving past.
     Our police car stayed with us then, a while still.

I couldn't see, (& forgot
to look when he pulled off,)
     but he must have been a state officer.

He took us at least as far as the next county line.

Then each of us, just those three or four cars,
turned up & headed off
     down the road on our ways.

The Ghost Train

Fast intent that a singular imprinting
the now-ghostly train itself — flesh made
at least one heartsick humanoid sound
pouring seeking through our black woods

well down absent light for spiral climbing
the dull wound-lumps of our great oak
as old as the Indians one hundred-fifty
foot dear & proud dark warrior pausing

at a boy's southern window dripping
slow single tears which froze like acorns
when they struck hard roof rattling demons
over the other tree-junk back into calm

& that space for me alone to witness —
some cry which you (a friend) & I would
certainly chase down certainly nipping one
of our feet on a jade chunk of Coke glass

just then dousing it in the shivering creek —
how primal that barbed wire before the stone
tunnel cast beneath the phantom tracks! &
who might have only in passing physically

spike by spike drawn up the dead sleepers
released our bikes but crude reincarnations
in the gravel lot up at the Catholic ballfields
that we — you me one of my sisters I think —

must've hidden a while in wound up in –
her little circus act for your applause where
the thrilling moment prior I had fishtailed
us in on a swell of thick pale dust &

cowered with you beneath the window
begging it would settle again for a cop car?

L'Amour des Hommes

(The Love of Men)

For no (good, reasonable) reason
   My little brother & me just blew
Up, tossed a couple joking & then
   Rabid-ass fists & a chair – threw

That fricking barstool, pinned me
   A second & jammed my goddamn
Hip socket – he's like, *Sorry*, sorry
   Sorry, sorry & I tore up after him

& Then bruised the f*ck out of my
   Wrist almost beating down my dad's
Door where he ran – don't forget: I
   Chased you, don't forget you made

Me grab you at your car & don't
   Forget with what control I talked
     You all the way back inside to sleep
With me, not for anything – *I won't*,
   I said, just to sleep with me, *please*,
   (In my bed, his door was locked.)

J. T. Welsch

Pere Marquette State Park

. . . ago in the land of the Alton
Giant, we spent an afternoon once,
my family, my uncle Russ
joking about giant tree snakes

that would fall on us – *look out!*
he dropped his arms around
my little sister's shoulders
& we all screamed.

My grandpa was born & lived there
till he told his math teacher
to 'go to hell' after being
accused of cheating.

(He never showed his workings,
just had a memory like that –
came in handy remembering serial numbers
for used car parts later.)

He wadded up the test & ate it,
stormed out of school, lied about his age
& joined the navy,
ended up on a minesweeper
off the coast of Okinawa
when they surrendered.

'Oh,' Was the Sound of the Waiting Room

Oh, was the sound of the waiting room
once I'd burst in, dripping from the rain,
& excused myself – holding our dachshund,

shivering in my sweatshirt in my arms –
ahead of the line at the front desk.

My mom called you, I told her quietly.
She swallowed pills, she needs her stomach pumped.
(This was when some of them said, *Oh,* softly.)

The doctor came & I handed her off,
within my sweatshirt, into his keeping.

. . .

She was fine though. I don't really know
if it makes their sympathy less needed,
but she's fine. It's a complicated thing,

(like most things. I'm sure it's not unique.)
The real trouble was with our labrador.

First, we're sure now she didn't eat the pills,
(the dachshund must've & just been fine,)
but we thought we'd just check both dogs.

Then in the hurry, I forgot the leash
& had to drag her by her neck scuff

across the little gravel lot, stopping
at every puddle to get a drink.
(This is a big dog I'm talking about.)

It was a hurry, but she was in charge.
I could only tug so hard on her skin.

. . .

The doctor spoke very frankly with us:
This does not look like a well dog to me.
We drove her back the next morning for tests.

By then, we'd ruled out the pills for certain,
& her 'arthritis' was beside the point –

just like that, she could barely move her head.
A week before, she'd seemed completely fine.
She had looked fine. She laid around a lot,

but she had always laid around a lot.
Now she could barely even lift her head.

Her eyes were so pale, she wouldn't eat.
They did blood tests to confirm themselves –
it was some sort of immune disorder.

Her own cells were attacking her inside.
She must've had it a few months now –

. . .

I leashed the dachshund & met my mom there,
to see her & to make the decision.
I don't think she was in pain, she lay still

after trying to sit when she heard us.
The doctor smiled for our sakes when her tail

moved under his ratty blue blanket.
He told us everything, then left us alone.
I wouldn't say we stood in there too long.

My mom & I both cried, the dachshund
mostly just nosed around the equipment.

. . .

Katy was perfectly coherent.
She wasn't in pain, but I thought she
looked miserable.
                    It's not like a person,

it's not like we can just say, 'Come on, now,'
or just ask her what she wants, Mom whispered.

. . .

I was 13-years-old & thought, fiercely:
Why do we attack ourselves so stupidly?
Why bother to pull something in so close,

& fool ourselves into loving something – like
look, look at this piece of the world I can love!

J. T. Welsch

I will make myself watch it run away.
I'll wait & have it ripped from my hands,
in my lifetime, because . . . I live forever!

I just go on & on, watching things die,
all around me, all passing through my love,

thinking I can swap one for the other,
(but name them, keep them distinct to hurt worst,
so every trade can be the hardest death.)

*Don't look at me, Katy, just lay back down.
We have to leave you here now, okay? Bye.*

Footnotes to an Elegy

I am always begging myself to trust
that fear is of a gentlest purpose

at heart, or that the deep suffering or
pain of a beloved human creature

(which gives me the strongest sensation
of that fear,) at some point culminates in

something which I will then be able
to accept as perfectly beautiful.

When so frequently I fail at this,
there is of course the opposite stance,

wherein I beg myself to review
& dismiss these things as one mortal flaw,

see that fear or belovedness itself
is something for which I am liable,

thus expected to rein in, as it were,
if only I was somehow stronger.

J. T. Welsch

Yet, as surely as I lack the strength
or confidence for any true faith,

I find I am without the will for true
skepticism, & wind up much too

often self-abandoned in the great
openness between, where I am afraid

that fear, whether contrived by myself
or elsewhere, is the most believable.

The Well Witcher

Grandpa Thiele (hands pictured
here) was, I just learned, a witcher
of wells, & a good one
at that: *upwards 100 a year*, article says. Died when
I was 6 & he's 97, but I got a memory
taken, I'll admit, more from a story

Mom still tells than fact:
him holding our spayed cat
Molsen (named for a food-bowl misprint)
barking *Ach! Is pregnant!*
Dad, rereading over my shoulder, recollected, this
afternoon after Grandma H's

funeral, going along once, how Grandpa Thiele
had him touch his hands & feel
the pulses from the forked limb in these
wrinkled palms – joked my sister
or I *might have the gift* – smiled about his
grandfather showing him where

even branches on the trees bend together
toward the buried water.